THE
LOST DISCIPLINE
THAT WILL
CHANGE YOUR LIFE

PRAYER

THE
LOST DISCIPLINE
THAT WILL
CHANGE YOUR LIFE

PRAYER

MICHAEL ROSS

BARBOUR BOOKS
An Imprint of Barbour Publishing, Inc.

CONTENTS

ACKNOWLEDGMENTS

I am deeply grateful to an amazing team that helped make this book a reality:

Arnie Cole EdD (Pepperdine)—CEO of Back to the Bible, an international radio and internet ministry. In addition, he is the Director of Research and Development for the Center for Bible Engagement. Arnie has spent much of his professional life tracking trends of human behavior. He is the coauthor of seven books, including *Seven Secrets of Worry-Free Living* (BroadStreet Publishing). Arnie and his wife, Char, are parents of adult children and operate an equestrian center in Nebraska.

Pamela Ovwigho, PhD—Executive Director of the Center for Bible Engagement, a division of Back to the Bible. She has spent the past eight years analyzing the spiritual lives of more than 170,000 people. When she's not asking people questions, Pam is busy fixing up the one-hundred-year-old Nebraska farmhouse she shares with her husband and children. She directed all of the research that became the foundation of this book and contributed to chapter 1.

Tiffany Ross, MDiv—writer, videographer, and children's ministry pastor. She has authored or coauthored six books—including *101 Ways to Strengthen the Parent-Child Connection* (goTandem/Barbour)—and is a former film production coordinator at Focus on the Family. Tiffany graduated cum laude from Nazarene Theological Seminary in Kansas City and served as an officer in the United States Army National Guard. She and her husband, Michael, live in Lincoln, Nebraska, with their son Christopher. She contributed to chapters 3 and 7.

Vanessa Janusz—writer, ministry leader, and loving wife. She gave her heart to Jesus at age seven, grew up in West Virginia, and is committed to being Christ's "hands and feet" to the people of Long Island, New York—where she ministers with her husband, Walt. Vanessa is passionate about prayer and trains others in how to get the most out of this "discipline that will change your life." She contributed to chapter 13.

Greg Asimakoupoulos—writer and senior pastor in suburban Seattle. He is the author of nine books (including *Heroic Faith: How to Live a Life of Extreme Devotion*) and is married with three children. He contributed to chapter 2.

Margie Younce—Program director for a nonprofit organization for children and their families in West Virginia. Along with her husband, Pete, Margie is a worship leader at her church. She contributed to Chapter 12.

Introduction

"LORD, TEACH US TO PRAY"

Once Jesus was in a certain place praying. As he finished, one of
his disciples came to him and said, "Lord, teach us to pray, just as
John taught his disciples." Jesus said, "This is how you should pray:
Father, may your name be kept holy. May your Kingdom come soon.
Give us each day the food we need, and forgive us our sins, as we
forgive those who sin against us. And don't let us yield to temptation."

LUKE 11:1–4 NLT

Prayer was the breath that Jesus breathed, the driving force of
His life, the secret of His amazing ministry.[1] He modeled a
perfect prayer life, and He encouraged His disciples to never stop
praying. "But when you pray, go away by yourself, shut the door
behind you, and pray to your Father in private. Then your Father,
who sees everything, will reward you. When you pray, don't
babble on and on as the Gentiles do. They think their prayers
are answered merely by repeating their words again and again"
(Matthew 6:6–7 NLT).

As Jesus traveled throughout Judea and beyond, ministering
everywhere He went, the disciples saw the place of prayer in His
life. And the more time they spent with Him, the more they
caught His teaching on the importance of a persistent prayer life.

Jesus prayed in public, and He prayed alone; He prayed for
the young and the old alike. He prayed during joyful moments,
and He prayed during times of trouble.

Jesus prayed often—*everywhere* and in *every* situation:

- while speaking to crowds of people (Matthew 11:25–26)

- before He walked on water (Matthew 14:23)
- as He interacted with little children (Matthew 19:13–15)
- during the Last Supper (Matthew 26:26)
- in Gethsemane before He was betrayed (Matthew 26:36–44)
- as He was dying on the cross (Matthew 27:46)
- before He traveled to Galilee (Mark 1:35–36)
- as He healed a deaf and mute man (Mark 7:31–35)
- at His baptism (Luke 3:21–22)
- after healing people (Luke 5:16)
- all night long before He selected His disciples (Luke 6:12–13)
- before Peter called Jesus "the Christ" (Luke 9:18)
- during His transfiguration (Luke 9:28–29)
- when He was filled with the joy of the Holy Spirit (Luke 10:21)
- before He taught the Lord's Prayer (Luke 11:1)
- as He prayed for Peter's faith (Luke 22:31–32)
- right after He was nailed to the cross (Luke 23:34)
- during His dying breath (Luke 23:46)
- when He broke bread after His resurrection (Luke 24:30)
- as He blessed His disciples before ascending into heaven (Luke 24:50–53)
- before He fed a crowd of five thousand people (John 6:11)
- before He raised Lazarus from the dead (John 11:41–42)
- while He asked the Father to bring glory to God's name (John 12:27–28)
- as He considered His mission, as well as the faith and work of His disciples and all believers (John 17:1–26)

If prayer was an essential part of Christ's life, shouldn't it be the same for us? Prayer keeps us trusting God for everything, opens the way for the Holy Spirit to transform us into the image of Jesus, and enables God to touch the lives of others whom we meet.[2]

Yet, too often, prayer is lacking in a believer's life.

Too often, prayer is the "lost discipline."

"Where we should be the strongest, we're the weakest," author and internationally renowned speaker Kay Arthur observes. "Is this why so many who profess Christ live such impotent and ordinary lives? Why so many people, even those who have been 'well-known' in the Western world of Christianity, have 'fallen into sin'?"[3]

Our own research at Back to the Bible has uncovered both the power of prayer and the tragic consequences when believers avoid it. And every day we receive dozens of letters from Christ-followers who desire a better prayer life but just don't know how to achieve it.

"My prayer life has never been what it needs to be," wrote Keith, a forty-two-year-old from Pennsylvania. "I feel like the act of prayer can be so stiff—so 'holier-than-thou.' You have to achieve this certain stage in order to come to God. For me, my prayers vary. Sometimes I talk out loud while I'm driving. Sometimes I pray silently to the Lord. A lot of times in my heart, I'm yelling. A lot of times, I'm begging. And the Lord just keeps loving. He is 'God with Me.' He is here and now. The Lord is near to the brokenhearted. He is closer to me now than ever before in my life."

Ready for real transformation? Let's ask the same question the disciples took to Jesus: "Lord, teach us to pray." We'll take our curiosity straight to God's Word, and together we'll uncover secrets of "the lost discipline that will change your life."

And as you read these pages, keep in mind three truths:

1. God delights in our prayers. He longs to demonstrate His power in the tremendous trials that shake the foundation of our lives, as well as in the tiny troubles that annoy us. Giant needs are never too great for His power; small ones are never too insignificant for His love.

2. God answers prayer because He is the supreme ruler of all. He governs both world events and our individual lives, ready at our request to act, to intervene, to overrule for our good, His glory, and the progress of the Gospel.

3. God moves through prayer. Not only are we called to this divine activity (Philippians 4:6 and 1 Timothy 2:1–3), but we are guaranteed of God's action in response to our prayers. And as 2 Chronicles 7:14 clearly states, if we pray, God promises results. He has assured us that prayer is the way to secure His aid and to move His mighty hand. Therefore, even in sickness, failure, rejection, or financial distress, we can pray and experience His peace. "Have faith in God," Jesus said. "Truly I tell you, if anyone says to this mountain, 'Go, throw yourself into the sea,' and does not doubt in their heart but believes that what they say will happen, it will be done for them" (Mark 11:22–23).

Let's get started. . . .

PART ONE

PRAYER BASICS

1

A PEEK INSIDE YOUR CLOSET: PRAYER LIVES OF EVERYDAY CHRISTIANS

*Devote yourselves to prayer with
an alert mind and a thankful heart.*

COLOSSIANS 4:2 NLT

On any given day, we encounter multiple opportunities to pray for others. Sometimes specific requests for prayer come through conversations, other times via email, text, or even social media. They come from family, friends, coworkers, acquaintances, and even, at times, complete strangers.

We're not surprised by how often people request prayer. Every day at Back to the Bible, we receive hundreds of prayer requests. Life can be tough and each of us encounters those storms in which we need help. No, what surprises us is who the requests come from. We've had practicing Christians, practicing Muslims, Hindus, agnostics, and even those who are functional atheists ask us to pray for them or for someone they love.

It appears there's a nearly universal tendency for people to pray (or at least petition prayer from others). If you ask just about anyone, "How do you communicate with God?" you'll receive one answer: *prayer*. In a recent survey of adults in the United States between the ages of eighteen and twenty-nine, we found that 80 percent believe in prayer. Our twenty-country study from several years ago looked at how often people from different religions pray. In a typical week, 90 percent of Muslims, 86 percent of

Hindus, 77 percent of Christians, 47 percent of Buddhists, and 46 percent of Jews will pray.[1]

Scientists have also noticed the popularity of prayer. A survey in the early 2000s found that prayer was the most commonly named alternative health treatment in the US.[2] Another study of critical care nurses revealed that prayer is very common in their circles as well. Eight out of ten reported having been asked by patients or their families to pray, and the same proportion have recommended prayer to patients.[3]

It's not surprising then that prayer has become a topic of research. In this chapter—with the help of Dr. Pam Ovwigho, executive director of the Center for Bible Engagement at Back to the Bible—we'll take a closer look at two areas of that research: Christians' prayer practices and the effects of prayer.

What's Going On in That Prayer Closet?

As I (Pam) walk into my church sanctuary, the usher hands me a small piece of paper. One side provides the outline of the upcoming sermon. The other lists our congregation's prayer needs. In our church of more than two thousand men, women, and children, this list is quite long. We pray for these needs during the worship service. Our pastor also encourages us to pray for them during the week in our own private devotional time.

If I'm truthful, more often than not this list generates guilt for me. Although I do take time to pray each day, I'm not always diligent about praying for my local church needs.

I wonder if I'm the only one who falls into this category. My parents, in contrast, are all about praying for their fellow congregants. They each keep a lengthy list, praying over and updating it regularly. In addition, they are a link in the church's emergency prayer chain. I've witnessed this chain in action many times. The phone will ring, and usually my mom will answer and take down the information. When she hangs up, she and Dad will pray immediately. It doesn't matter what they were doing before the phone rang. Everything stops until they have lifted the need to the Lord.

What about you? Have you ever wondered what other believers' prayer lives are like? If so, this is the chapter for you! Over the years we have surveyed more than two hundred thousand people about all aspects of their spiritual lives. Let's take a look at what we've learned about how they talk to God.

Importance and Frequency

One way we peek into believers' spiritual lives is by asking them to rate on a five-point scale how important different spiritual practices are to them. Typically, prayer receives the highest ranking for importance, slightly higher than worship and Bible engagement.

Using the same scale, I also like to ask folks how satisfied they are with the way they are living out the different spiritual practices. Satisfaction ratings are generally lower than the importance ratings. This is true for prayer as well, with an average "satisfaction" rating of 3.16 but importance of 4.84. The gap between these numbers is bigger than for other spiritual practices, suggesting that this may be an area where many of us struggle.

We mentioned earlier that most people pray at least sometimes. How regularly does your average Christian? Through our many church surveys, we've found that about two-thirds of Christians pray daily. The remaining third will pray on two or more days in a typical week.

Most often this is individual prayer. However, among married couples, most (64 percent) also pray together during the week.

How We Pray

What struck me most about the movie *The War Room* were the scenes of the various characters in their "prayer closets." Sometimes they were sitting or standing. Other times they were kneeling or even lying on the floor. Hands were clenched or raised at times. In those closets, prayers were silent, whispered, spoken, and shouted.

On top of the many alternatives for posture and tone, we also have an endless list of options when it comes to the content of our prayers. We may choose to recite a psalm or another passage of God's Word. We may praise God for who He is, thank Him for what He's done, confess our sins, ask for forgiveness, seek wisdom and guidance, and share the concerns weighing on our hearts.

So which among these choices are the most common? Through our surveys we have learned that most people

- pray for someone else;
- ask for God's help in a particular situation;
- express thanks or gratitude;
- ask for help in changing something about themselves; or
- pray about the wrong things they've done.

Only about half of us (53 percent) regularly recite composed prayers. About the same amount say that they pray because they feel like it's an obligation.

While these are the most common patterns, it's important to remember that our Lord doesn't limit us. Each time we pray, we may use the posture, tone, and topics most fitting for the circumstances.

The Difference Prayer Makes. . .at Least According to Science

> *The LORD is near to all who call on him, to all who call on him in truth. He fulfills the desire of those who fear him; he also hears their cry and saves them.*
> PSALM 145:18–19 ESV

> *Therefore, confess your sins to one another and pray for one another, that you may be healed. The prayer of a righteous person has great power as it is working. Elijah was a man with a nature like ours, and he prayed fervently that it might not rain, and for three years and six months it did not rain on the earth. Then he prayed again, and heaven gave rain, and the earth bore its fruit.*
> JAMES 5:16–18 ESV

The other major area of prayer research, focused on what a difference prayer makes, engenders a good amount of controversy. The verses listed above proclaim the truth that the Lord hears our cries and that prayer has great power. Because we know that our God is omnipotent, we are confident that He has the power to heal and transform our minds, bodies, relationships, and world.

However, these spiritual truths play out in various ways in

reality. Sometimes God answers our prayers with a "yes," other times a "no," and often a "wait." Our understanding of how God has responded to our prayer may come immediately. Other times we don't recognize the Lord's answer until days, weeks, or even years later.

All of these factors make it a bit messy when we then try to bring prayer into the lab. The most common types of studies have examined the effect of intercessory prayer on healing. They usually adopt a triple-blind design meaning that (1) the patients being prayed for don't know someone is praying for them; (2) the intercessors don't have contact with the patients; and (3) the medical treatment team is not aware of which patients are being prayed for and which are not.

Dozens of studies have examined, in this experimental setting, whether intercessory prayer made a difference in health outcomes for people with conditions such as diabetes, heart problems, and more. While some individual studies have shown positive effects from prayer, analyses considering all of them together reveal no differences in health outcomes between the prayer group and the group that didn't have the research team interceding for them.[4]

How do we reconcile our confidence that God answers prayer with scientific evidence that intercessory prayer doesn't statistically improve health outcomes? I believe there are two excellent explanations. First, there is no guarantee in these experiments that no one was praying for the people in the control group. We only know they weren't being prayed for by the intercessors in the experiment. Given how common prayer is, it's perfectly reasonable to conclude that a good many of them were being prayed for by their family and friends.

A second explanation is one we touched on earlier: our Lord always answers prayers, but not always in the way we expect. There are times when we pray for physical healing and that person instead goes to their eternal home. There are times when we pray for a marriage to last and the couple ends up divorced instead. The multiple possible outcomes of intercessory prayer make it impossible to put God in the proverbial box of statistical prediction.

Although research has failed to demonstrate how intercessory prayer works, it has provided considerable evidence of benefits for the person praying. Dr. Andrew Newberg, a neuroscientist at Thomas Jefferson University and Hospital, has spent the past two decades studying how religious experiences affect our brains. His fascinating studies have been published in scientific journals and the popular press and have even been featured on television news shows. His work shows that people who pray over many years have thicker and more active frontal lobes than nonpractitioners.[5] Interestingly, the frontal lobes are known as the "control panel" of our personality and are central to our ability to communicate.

In addition to these brain changes, science also shows that prayer has these five benefits:[6]

1. *Prayer improves self-control.* Like a muscle, we can strengthen our ability to control our impulses. Science shows that prayer helps to build up our self-control "muscles."
2. *Prayer makes us gentler.* People who pray for others are less likely to use aggression when something angers them.

3. *Prayer helps us forgive.* Praying for a loved one or friend makes us more willing to forgive them.
4. *Prayer increases trust.* Matthew 18:20 tells us that Jesus will be among us whenever two or more of us gather in his name. Science now shows the power of praying in community. When we pray with a friend, we increase the trust and sense of unity between us.
5. *Prayer diminishes the negative health effects of stress.* In an interesting study of older adults, researchers found that praying for others reduced the stress of chronic financial problems. A key part here is the focus on others. Praying for one's own material well-being did not reduce stress and its health effects.

Our survey respondents have also shared how prayer affects them. For example, 60 percent frequently feel that God is responding to their prayers. Two out of three frequently feel a sense of peace when they pray, and 75 percent believe that prayer can affect how things turn out.

⟆

For many believers, what science does or doesn't say about prayer is little more than trivia. They know that God's Word tells us the importance and power of prayer, and that is all the information they need.

While we wholeheartedly agree that the Bible is our source of truth about prayer, we also believe that He has given us curious minds and that the scientific method is possibly one way we can learn more. Many of the prayer studies get discussed in the local news. When we are aware of them, we can use them as a jumping-off point for deeper conversations about what prayer is, what it is not, and how important it is to our lives. We hope this chapter has helped you consider your own prayer life more deeply.

2

BUT GOD RARELY SHOWS UP. . .SO WHY PRAY?

"Oh, that you would bless me and expand my territory!
Please be with me in all that I do, and keep me from all trouble and pain!"
1 CHRONICLES 4:10 NLT

My God, my God, why have you abandoned me?
Why are you so far away when I groan for help?
PSALM 22:1 NLT

Two men, two prayers—two very different results. . .

The first comes from 1 Chronicles 4:9–10, in which a man named Jabez boldly asked God for a good life—one free of trouble and pain. Amazingly, God gave him what he asked for.

Scripture tells us that Jabez was "more honorable than his brothers," yet according to Bible scholars, his name sounds like a Hebrew word that means "distress" or "pain." Some experts surmise that his birth must have brought physical or emotional pain to his mother, so she named him "Jabez"—predicting her boy's challenging future. In ancient times, a person's name often defined their lot in life or who they might become. Jabez obviously beat the odds. He apparently believed in the power of God and prayed with urgency and vulnerability. In return, the Lord brought favor on his life.

The second prayer is from King David and is recorded in Psalm 22.

David's prayer was equally gutsy, yet it had nothing to do

with his desire for prosperity or blessings. . .or a pain-free existence. For David, pain *was* the problem. He felt as if he had gotten a raw deal from God, and he wanted some answers: "Why have you abandoned me? Look at what has happened—I'm so miserable. Why all this cruelty? Why the silence?"

Even though David cried out again and again, God remained silent.

I (Arnie) admire the boldness of both men, yet in all honesty, I relate more to David. His circumstances raise an important question that I've pondered in different seasons of my life: What should we do when God doesn't show up?

What happens when the Lord doesn't seem to answer our prayers—when we suffer, when we beg for deliverance. . .yet all we feel is silence? Should we stop praying altogether? Should we stop believing that prayer makes a difference? Absolutely *not*!

Even when life is caving in around us, we have to be honest with God. We have to cry out to Him just as David did. Take a look at verses 1–2 of Psalm 22 (NLT):

> *My God, my God, why have you abandoned me?*
> *Why are you so far away when I groan for help?*
> *Every day I call to you, my God, but you do not answer.*
> *Every night I lift my voice, but I find no relief.*

If you think those words have a familiar ring, you're right. Jesus repeated some of those very words as He hung on the cross, dying for our sins. But they weren't original with Jesus. Israel's most famous king said them first. But as we keep reading in Psalm 22 (verses 11–18 NLT), we see how closely David's metaphorical description of his personal crisis fits the passion of

Christ. Can you just hear Jesus saying the following?

> *Do not stay so far from me, for trouble is near,*
> *and no one else can help me. My enemies surround*
> *me like a herd of bulls; fierce bulls of Bashan have*
> *hemmed me in! Like lions they open their jaws*
> *against me, roaring and tearing into their prey.*
> *My life is poured out like water, and all my bones*
> *are out of joint. My heart is like wax, melting*
> *within me. My strength has dried up like sunbaked*
> *clay. My tongue sticks to the roof of my mouth. You*
> *have laid me in the dust and left me for dead. My*
> *enemies surround me like a pack of dogs; an evil*
> *gang closes in on me. They have pierced my hands*
> *and feet. I can count all my bones. My enemies stare*
> *at me and gloat. They divide my garments among*
> *themselves and throw dice for my clothing.*

David's enemies were out to get him, and he felt completely alone. As far as the king was concerned, God had forgotten all about him. In David's frontline battle to maintain control of his kingdom, the Creator of the cosmos was missing in action. No "prayer of Jabez" answers here. In fact, there were no apparent answers at all to David's prayers. God was silent, and His actions seemed so unfair. All the same, in this pessimistic psalm, David offers us some suggestions about how to pray when we feel as if God just isn't showing up.

Expect the Worst

When David prayed Psalm 22, he was in serious trouble. The happy days he'd experienced earlier in his life were a distant memory. This day was bleak because of people who were out to get him. He wasn't sure he'd live to see tomorrow.

No doubt we all know what it's like to be on the ropes. Friends betray. Pets die. Marriages fail. Jobs end. Bank accounts dry up. And in the midst of it all, sometimes we feel abandoned by God. We cry out in anguish yet experience nothing but silence.

Life on a sin-marred planet is marked by setbacks such as these. Expect them. David learned to. The episode that prompted Psalm 22 was only one of many in the king's life.

Disregard Feelings

On occasion—especially during tough times—we may not sense God in our lives and feel as if He is far away from us. But keep in mind that we haven't been saved by "feelings." Accept the Lord by faith as a *fact*. As Christ-followers, we have Jesus living within us every second of every day. The Reverend Billy Graham reminds us, "He is living in you in order to magnify, glorify, and exalt Christ in you so that you can live a happy, victorious, radiant, and Christ-honoring life."[1] Never lose sight of this truth.

Keep Talking

David is convinced that God has abandoned him. But does he quit praying? Not at all! In fact, he continues to pour out his heart to a God he isn't quite sure is listening to him. This is what's known as faith. You act on what you know is true even when you don't have much evidence.

One of the marks of a growing Christian is the

determination to look toward the Son even when He seems to be hidden by dark clouds. Remain in contact with the One you've committed your life to. Act as though He's listening even when you can't tell whether He is. Talk to the Lord every day. Long speeches aren't necessary.

Don't Fake It

Be honest. How do you feel about the fact that David is secure enough in his friendship with the Lord to be completely honest with his feelings? Isn't it kind of cool that he wants God to know he's disillusioned and jaded? Can't you just hear him? "Life has gotten pretty lousy. Where has trusting You gotten me anyway?" Okay, so David doesn't say exactly that. But he does pray despite how he feels.

"My God, my God, why have you abandoned me? Why are you so far away when I groan for help? . . . You have laid me in the dust and left me for dead" (Psalm 22:1–2, 15 NLT).

When we feel shortchanged by God, we shouldn't pretend as if we like it. Instead, we need to talk it out. We need to tell Him how we feel: abandoned, misunderstood, or taken advantage of. The Lord can handle whatever it is we feel inside. He won't be put off by what we say. The fact that David's prayer is in the Bible means God wants us to communicate our deepest doubts and rawest anger even if we feel He's let us down. (And just in case we've forgotten, the Lord is capable of reading our minds and knows if our pious words are for real).

Be Patient

As you read Psalm 22, compare the way David starts with the way he ends. Do you notice a difference? By the time David has finished unloading on God, his perspective has changed. God is back in view. David is on His side. Take a look at verses 23–28 (NLT):

> Praise the LORD, all you who fear him! Honor him, all you descendants of Jacob! Show him reverence, all you descendants of Israel! For he has not ignored or belittled the suffering of the needy. He has not turned his back on them, but has listened to their cries for help.
>
> I will praise you in the great assembly. I will fulfill my vows in the presence of those who worship you. The poor will eat and be satisfied. All who seek the LORD will praise him. Their hearts will rejoice with everlasting joy. The whole earth will acknowledge the LORD and return to him. All the families of the nations will bow down before him. For royal power belongs to the LORD. He rules all the nations.

Notice the complete change of heart? It sounds as if someone else is on his knees before the heavenly Father. The dark clouds are gone. The sky is clear. Feelings of being forsaken have been forgotten. David is back on track with God.

It's hard to know how much time David's prayer represents. Chances are, the prayer that is recorded in Psalm 22 wasn't prayed in one sitting (or kneeling). The time between what was going on at the beginning of the prayer and at the ending could have been weeks or months. But it is likely that David kept talking to God about his situation the whole time.

In other words, even if it feels as if God hasn't shown up, don't give up.

Never stop trusting God—or praying—just because the landscape hasn't changed overnight. It may take longer than we think. But then again, simply telling God about our problems may help us see aspects of the Lord's character that we've forgotten.

As this prayer by David illustrates, honest communication with God is a great way to process what is going on in our lives. It's a healthy way to work through what we're feeling, as well as to confide our greatest fears and highest hopes to the Lord.

Laments and "Where are You, God?" style prayers verbalize the grunt-hard difficulties and disappointments of life in a way that reminds us that there is no situation we face that God is not interested in.[2]

When Good Christians and Hard Times Collide. . .

Maybe our faith is being tested. "The Father never tempts His children to do evil," observes author and radio Bible teacher Warren W. Wiersbe. "However, He does test our faith, because a faith that can't be tested can't be trusted. Faith is only as good as the object of that faith, and our faith is in the one true and living God. . . . Whenever anyone makes a profession of faith in Jesus Christ, they will soon enter a time of trial and testing so they can learn whether or not their faith is real."[3]

Maybe God is saving us from our own arrogance. "Overconfidence seems to be a big deal to God," explains Sarah Lebhar Hall, an adjunct professor of biblical studies at Gordon-Conwell Theological Seminary and Trinity School for Ministry. "It's something to be avoided at all costs. It poses a serious danger to our souls. Look at the lengths God goes to in order to help His people avoid it. Gideon's army is shrunk. Paul's 'thorn' is allowed to persist. God permits dramatic challenges in our lives, a significant reduction of our resources, in order to save us from arrogance."[4]

Maybe it's just a fact of life. "The question of why some prayers seem to be answered and others don't has plagued theologians for centuries," writes author Tony Jones in his book *Pray.* "Trials and temptations are a part of life. . . . They help us remember to rely on God; otherwise we tend to go our own way."[5]

3

HOW PRAYER WORKS

But when you ask, you must believe and not doubt, because the one who doubts is like a wave of the sea, blown and tossed by the wind.

JAMES 1:6 NIV

Prayer is connection. "The LORD is near to all who call on him, to all who call on him in truth. He fulfills the desires of those who fear him; he hears their cry and saves them" (Psalm 145:18–19).

Prayer is communion. "If you love me, keep my commands. And I will ask the Father, and he will give you another advocate to help you and be with you forever" (John 14:15–16).

Prayer is conversation. *"Be anxious for nothing, but in everything by prayer and supplication, with thanksgiving, let your requests be made known to God; and the peace of God, which surpasses all understanding, will guard your hearts and minds through Christ Jesus"* (Philippians 4:6–7 NKJV).

Prayer is critical. In the words of R. C. Sproul:

> *The Lord God of the universe, the Creator and Sustainer of all things. . .not only commands us to pray, but also invites us to make our requests known. . . . In the act and dynamic of praying, I bring my whole life under His gaze. Yes, He knows what is in my mind, but I still have the privilege of articulating to Him what is there. He says, "Come. Speak to Me. Make your requests known to Me." And so, we come in order to know Him and to be known by Him.*[1]

Several years back, I (Michael) had hit a spiritual low point in my walk with Christ. I felt burned out, stressed out, and stuck. And when uncertainty knocked on the door, I hid behind the couch. Then I'd readjust my mask and pretend like everything was okay.

At the time, I headed up a youth magazine for a large Christian ministry. I had been in my position for about twenty years and genuinely loved my job. I got to wear many hats: journalist, author, speaker, product developer, event dreamer, creative team leader. I got to travel and meet interesting people from all walks of life. I got to write books and speak on the radio as a youth culture expert.

Yet through the years I'd become comfortable, and little by little, I was becoming distracted. (My job title began to swallow up my identity.) What had happened to the *real* person inside: child of God, servant of the Most High. . .Christ-follower?

I was once the guy who worked with street kids in Los Angeles. I cared about the broken, the lonely, the homeless. I stood strong against racism and lived among and worked with people of different cultures. Somehow, I'd become soft and sheltered. Why was I content hanging out in the lofty towers of a religious fortress?

A few months later, after hosting a father-son event in Colorado, a fellow speaker and our camp's worship leader took me aside: "Mike, some of the other guys and I have been talking about you, and we believe God wants us to pray for you."

"Pray? For *me*—what?!" I'd just finished leading three hundred men and boys in prayer. I was the ministry leader. . .and they wanted to pray for me.

"Yeah, we all sense that you're really struggling inside," my friend told me. "You're holding on, and God wants you to let go. You're trapped and full of fear, and you haven't learned to fully trust Him. And that, my pal, is nothing short of sin. Your future success in ministry hinges on steps you take right now."

"*What?!* Let go. . .sin. . .my future?"

My heart was racing and my hands were trembling. How could they possibly know these things about me? (I thought I'd done a pretty good job of masking my pain.) This was starting to feel like some sort of spiritual confrontation. And when somebody says, "God told me something about your future," well, that freaks me out. I'd normally run—but there they were, surrounding me, laying hands on me. I was trapped!

Suddenly, another shake-up: *Quit being phony. It's time to be real. It's time to surrender control. Let go.*

I prayed with the guys, cried a little, and confessed a few things: my lack of trust in God *and* people; my tendency to please others first, instead of the Lord; and, yes, my fear of uncertainty—especially about where Christ was leading me.

I wish I could say that I changed course that day, but I didn't. (It was more of a half-step.)

Not long afterward, with the mountains behind me, I slipped back into my routine—and the pressures and distractions of life. Call me hardheaded, call me a slow learner. . .I'm certain I'd fit right in with the grumbling Israelites Moses was trying to lead into the Promised Land! But one morning, as I was sitting in my office, I took a good look around and smiled. *I like this place. I like what I do. I like who I am. More importantly, I love my family. I'm really happy.* (In other words, I want to leave things just as they are because I'm too afraid to allow myself or my family to try something new.)

I bowed my head and began to pray: "I don't fully get what happened at the retreat or what to do with it. And frankly, the whole thing scares me. Thank You for this magazine and this ministry. Thank You for Your many blessings. Thank You for—"

"But are you challenged?"

I stopped in midsentence, opened my eyes, and looked around. I was alone, but I'm not exaggerating when I tell you that those words screamed through my brain like an audible voice.

Am I challenged? What does that mean?

And then another shake-up. Challenge was the last thing I was experiencing. My life was manageable. . .within my control. And that's how I liked things. But it really didn't matter what I preferred. If I'm serious about being a Christ-follower (let alone a ministry leader), it means that I can't pitch a tent in a comfort zone. God wants to move me along in my faith—on to deeper things, new challenges, more growth.

Whether I liked it or not, everything was about to change. . . .

Eighteen months after my mountaintop experience in Colorado, the economy went south. It was November 2008, and the mega-sized ship I called my place of employment had to downsize by 50 percent. My magazine was cut. . .and I was suddenly tossed out into a raging storm.

I was terrified.

There were more tears. . .and many, many more prayers.

As my family and I were heading home from church one Sunday morning, I knew God had come with His awakening hand and had grabbed me by the shoulders.

He did it through a tender question from my son: "Daddy, will you one day be in heaven with me?" *I was wrestling with doubt.*

He did it through a loving embrace from my wife: "You do know that things will be okay, don't you?" *I was weary and on the verge of spiritual burnout.*

He did it through the concern of my friend Lance: "How are you doing today—I mean really doing on the inside?" *I was afraid to be honest.*

He did it through scripture: "So, because you are lukewarm—neither hot nor cold—I am about to spit you out of my mouth" (Revelation 3:16). *I was disconnected from God. . .but I had a hard time admitting it.*

And then something that I never dreamed would happen, *actually happened.* I was okay. I even felt God's peace. He really could be trusted! (I'd established myself as an author, and the writing projects were coming in.)

A question I'd sensed Him asking earlier came back to me: "But are you challenged?"

No, Lord, I wasn't challenged. Instead, I was comfortable. Now I'm challenged and anything but comfortable.

Strangely, though, I felt more alive than ever. I was even excited—terrified, yet *excited.* It was time to move on to a whole new adventure.

So where are we headed now, Lord?

God took me places I never expected—back to a lost discipline in my life; back to fervent, believing prayer, and back to His Word. He took me right into the pages of the Bible, which I'd neglected in the past and so often misunderstood. (Instead, I relied too heavily on other people's opinions.)

I'll never forget what a friend once asked: "Have you ever read the Bible all the way through?"

I couldn't answer yes.

Then she went on to say, "I'm a Christ-follower, yet I haven't made the Bible a daily part of my life. And even though I pray, I feel like I'm just talking to myself. . .and that's pathetic. What if Christianity isn't what I think it is? What if it's better? What if my image of God isn't the right one? I really want the truth, so I'm trying not to read any other books as I focus on the Bible. And I'm going to take time to meditate on and pray through scripture. But mostly, I'm going to make an effort to stop, quiet my heart, and just listen to the Lord. I can't wait to hear what He has to say to me."

My friend's advice opened my eyes. She was talking about a powerful mix: prayer and Bible engagement. (More on this topic in chapter 5, "The Secret of Victorious Living.")

Suddenly, my faith was alive again. And the work God was doing in my life was transformational. Through His Word, through my community of believers, and through an active prayer life, He was leading me into a deeper relationship with Him. He was compelling me to *engage* His letters in the Bible with the passion of a lover. He was showing me how to find my Savior in the pages of scripture and how to have a daily walk with Jesus.

In the weeks and months that followed, the Lord rekindled a passion for prayer. Here's what He's teaching me. . . .

Tap Into the Power

As I know full well, life gets busy. Prayer has a way of getting bumped to a few quick words of thanks before we eat. Or it becomes a series of stress-induced pleas—as we face an agitated boss, a disappointed spouse, a disobedient child. How can our prayer lives be different? Better? Stronger? Characterized by more passion and power? How can we get back to the lost discipline that can change our lives?

The goal is to be in the presence of God. And we have been given this amazing ability to speak directly to the Creator of the universe. Stop and think about that for a minute. We, the created, have direct access to God, the Creator. Anytime, anywhere, we can have a conversation with our Lord. As we connect, the Spirit will guide us through our words and desires. But we have to admit it is sometimes difficult to spend time in prayer. We are tired, distracted, and feel rushed when we attempt to spend time with God. Even Jesus' closest friends couldn't stay awake as He prayed in the Garden of Gethsemane (Matthew 26:36–46). Jesus was distressed as He prayed that night. Three times he came back to His friends to find them asleep. So it's not just a struggle for the modern-day believer. People have always faced obstacles in their efforts to draw closer to God.

Pray Daily

Prayer is an investment in your relationship with God. Even though it is important to be prayerful in your thoughts throughout the day, quick little requests here and there are no substitute for a vibrant prayer life. But most of us have not been trained in how to pray. Sure, it's a conversation between us and our Creator. But it is also a time of searching, praising, and confessing. It is intimate and sometimes intense. This is how the Spirit shapes us as we draw closer to God. You may find it helpful to begin with a framework for your prayer time. The following is not a formula or a guaranteed path for a particular result. Instead, it is a way to intentionally place yourself in the presence of God. As you enter into a special time with our Lord, the Spirit will guide you through the rest. After all, the purpose of prayer is to connect with God, not merely complete a task or ritual.

Praise. Begin your time with God by acknowledging Him. Call Him by as many names as you can think of, such as "Abba, Father, Creator, Savior, King of Kings, Lion and Lamb, Master, Protector, All-Knowing," and so on. Recalling God's different attributes and roles helps us remember who we are praying to. It opens our minds to the many ways in which God works on our behalf. Praising and worshipping God is an interactive experience. It's both private and public. It involves both the heart and the head. And as we linger in God's presence, praising Him, we connect with the divine—the very Source of life. "Come near to God and he will come near to you" (James 4:8).

Thanks. Next, enter into a time of thanksgiving. Just like the old song says, "Count your blessings, name them one by one."[2] They don't have to be in any particular order; just let them roll out of your heart and mind as you remember how fortunate you are to be a child of God. Though it's easy to slip into other thoughts and requests, try to stay focused on thanksgiving. God deserves our thanks, so take time to linger in this moment. He delights in our prayers as we honor Him with our hearts and minds.

Confession. Chances are, you will be in a different state of mind after spending time praising and thanking God. You have focused on how magnificent God is while recognizing how special you are to Him. This is a special place that can draw you into a more honest experience with Him. As you humbly come before your Creator, you can let your defenses down and confess your sins. There is something powerful about admitting your mistakes. As you dig deeper, the Spirit takes you to the core of who you are. Sometimes you may be faced with difficult issues that are at the root of your struggles. Confession is freeing and sometimes emotional. It's not always easy, but God's continuing work in you is bringing you closer to Him. Remember, He is the One who creates new life in you. He is a mighty God who cares for you beyond measure, and He asks you to bring your private struggles to Him. As you hand them over to the One who can forgive, He restores your soul and His cleansing power shapes you into the person He has called you to be.

Petition. After you have had a moment of confession with God, turn your prayers toward your needs. It's possible that your request will be different after your time of confession. Your heart and mind will be more in line with God's desires. After recognizing God, thanking Him, and bringing your innermost struggles to light, your requests will be focused more on His will, not your own. The Lord wants to hear your needs and desires and also wants you to lift others up in prayer. He pulls you closer and closer to Him as your thoughts are shaped by the Spirit. And as your requests become more and more in line with God's desires, you will begin to gain a new vision of the world and of your significance to Him.

Submission. Just as Jesus prayed in the Garden of Gethsemane, seek God's will, not your own. This act of submission is powerful. It is a reminder that prayer is not a ritual of asking favors of a distant God but rather a personal connection with our Creator and Savior. He is on a mission and has included us in His plan. As we purposefully place ourselves in the presence of God, we are shaped by His desires and needs.

Seven Characteristics of Effective Prayer

1. *Humility.* According to legendary missionary and author Andrew Murray, humility is the soul of true prayer. "Until the spirit of the heart is renewed," he writes, "until it is emptied of all earthly desires and stands in a habitual hunger and thirst after God, which is the true spirit of prayer; until then, all our prayer will be more or less like lessons given to students. We will mostly say them only because we dare not neglect them."[3]

2. *Authenticity.* It's insane to think we can wear a mask or hide a secret when we approach God. He knows everything. "There is nothing concealed that will not be disclosed, or hidden that will not be made known. What you have said in the dark will be heard in the daylight, and what you have whispered in the ear in the inner rooms will be proclaimed from the roofs" (Luke 12:2–3). This is actually very good news because, while God knows every juicy detail of our lives, He still loves us desperately. He wants us to share everything with Him—our fears, our doubts, our anxieties, our struggles, our shame. . .*everything*.

3. *Belief.* As we pray, we can be confident that (1) God hears us, (2) He cares and knows what is best for us—remember, He sees the big picture—and (3) He is able to do anything and will answer our prayers according to His will and in His perfect time frame. "Now to him who is able to do immeasurably more than all we ask or imagine, according to his power that is at work within us, to him be glory in the church and in Christ Jesus throughout all generations, for ever and ever! Amen" (Ephesians 3:20–21).

4. *Surrender.* We can trust Jesus and let go of our burdens when we go to Him in prayer. And as the Spirit moves in our hearts, we'll begin to focus more on His love and His comfort. Our prayers will be shaped into moments of surrender that bring us closer to Him and His ways.

> *"Have faith in God," Jesus answered. "Truly
> I tell you, if anyone says to this mountain,
> 'Go, throw yourself into the sea,' and does not
> doubt in their heart but believes that what
> they say will happen, it will be done for them."*
> MARK 11:22–23

5. *Persistence.* This is for our sake, not God's. Persistence in prayer motivates us to work through an issue, and it compels us to get to the center of prayer—and right into the loving arms of our heavenly Father. Persistence draws us closer to God and nurtures our dependence on Him. "Man, created in the image of God, is meant to live in dependence upon his Creator," explains Christian scholar David Watson. "The essential nature of sin is independence: as I live my own life my own way, doing my own thing, God's image in me is blurred. For that image to be restored, I must turn from my sins, trust Jesus as my Savior, and live in total dependence upon God—a dependence marked by prayer."[4]

6. *Compassion.* This word means "suffering with" someone, feeling their pain and walking with them during times of trouble. Jesus was "moved with compassion" when He saw the needs of those around Him. God wants us to love others genuinely, help them in practical ways, and

pray with them and for them with compassion.

7. *Adoration.* We are to bring our requests to God with an attitude of thanksgiving, expecting that what awaits us is the peace of God that surpasses all understanding. And as we do so, we should give Him our praise and adoration—the spontaneous response of a grateful child of God in His presence. That's how Henry Blackaby describes it:

> *The person who knows God and experiences Him intimately sings to the Lord with deepest praise! Mary was overwhelmed by the Lord's goodness to her. In response, she sang one of the most beautiful and profound songs of praise found in Scripture. Trying to stop the praise of a thankful heart would be like trying to arrest the flow of a mighty waterfall! God created us to praise Him; praise will be our activity when we are gathered around His throne in heaven.*[5]

Anytime, Anywhere

The guidelines for prayer outlined in this chapter provide a way to come before our Lord intentionally with reverence and honesty. They remind us to remember who He is and the redemption He offers to the world.

But this outline is only a framework. It's not a special formula that guarantees anything. The Spirit is the One at work within us. And the Spirit will lead our prayers to the topics and struggles that will bring us closer to Him. These special moments with God mold us into believers who are more Christ-minded.

They help us to see the world as He would have us see it. And as we submit to His guidance, we are transformed.

Remember, the goal is to enter into the presence of God. So find a private moment—*anytime, anywhere*: during the wee hours of the morning, a moment in the middle of the day, at the side of your bed, at the kitchen table while everyone else is asleep, in an undisturbed corner of your house. Just stop, take a breath. . .and pray.

Our Lord Jesus often slipped away to be alone and to pray. Margaret Magdalen writes:

> *Jesus needed the silence of eternity as a thirsting man in the desert needs water. . . . He longed for time apart to bask and sunbathe in His Father's love, to soak in it and repose in it. No matter how drained He felt, it seems that this deep, silent communion refreshed Him more than a good night's sleep.*[6]

As we look to Christ as our example, we begin to recognize the amazing gift we have been given. Prayer is a direct link to the Source of all life—the same God who created us, loves us, redeems us, and acts on our behalf. And He has given us the ability to come directly to Him, *anytime, anywhere*.

PART TWO

UNLOCKING THE POWER OF PRAYER

4

CONFESSION: REGAINING INTIMACY WITH GOD

*So I find this law at work: Although I want to do good, evil is right there
with me. For in my inner being I delight in God's law; but I see another law
at work in me, waging war against the law of my mind and making me a
prisoner of the law of sin at work within me. What a wretched man I am!
Who will rescue me from this body that is subject to death? Thanks be to God,
who delivers me through Jesus Christ our Lord! So then, I myself in my mind
am a slave to God's law, but in my sinful nature a slave to the law of sin.*

ROMANS 7:21–25

> *It's late. Better stop. Well, a few more clicks. . .*
> *Wait—that can't be the time! I just checked the clock.*
> *Maybe I can't stop.*
> *Or maybe I'm just being uptight. It's not like I'm hurting anyone.*
> *And my life is stressful. This helps.*
> *But will God forgive me?*
> *What if my wife finds out? What if she already knows?*
> *Maybe I should stop. It's so late. Maybe too late. . .*

By the time Mark graduated from high school, he was living two
lives: one secret, one public. *It's like two different people are sharing
the same body,* he'd sometimes think. *I'm not sure which one is the
real me.*

What captivated his heart was also what he hated most—a
monster inside that was causing him to hate himself. Yet he
couldn't manage to break free.

At least no one knows.

On the surface, everything looked normal. Better than normal, actually—exceptional. Mark was handsome, athletic, and likable. He went to college in his hometown of St. Louis. He sang in his church choir and was unofficially nominated as the boy every mom wanted her daughter to marry.

He managed to convince himself that his life was good. Most days were routine, quietly compartmentalized—all within his control, just as he liked it. He learned how to cover his tracks, how to turn his emotions on and off, even how to dissociate himself from his own secret late-night activities.

Life is good, he'd tell himself, *and seems to be getting better and better.*

Mark loved Ashley, his high school sweetheart.[1] And when the two married, he promised to be faithful to her for his whole life.

"Nothing will ever come between us," he promised with a kiss. "I love you with all my heart. I *give* you my heart."

Within a few years, Ashley had her hands full with two energetic toddlers. Mark worked long hours to climb the corporate ladder, and he had big shoes to fill as VP of international sales. The stress was brutal, but his secret helped him to cope. (That is, that's how he justified his choices and actions.)

Porn had become a soothing, after-hours cocktail, one that turned into a distressing hangover the next morning.

"Why were you up so late—*again*?" Ashley wondered.

"Work, honey. And tons of it. You know the stress I'm under."

"It's always work. . .it's always something. What about me? What about our marriage?"

As much as this family man tried to deny what he was doing, and as much effort as he invested into suppressing what he was hiding, each connection with a voice on his cell phone or a video on his laptop was taking a relational toll. Mark was often too tired for real sex. Like white cotton soaking up black ink, his heart was becoming darker, more distorted. With each hit, the actual man was being replaced by a great pretender, someone who said the right words and smiled at the right times but was merely playing a part.

Mark was very much addicted, very much trapped, and not just to an image or a fantasy. He had a full-blown addiction to adrenaline—to taking a porn hit that delivered a feel-good signal whenever he decided he needed one.

One night at the dinner table, Ashley turned and locked eyes with Mark. *Late nights in the home office. No interest in romance. It's all beginning to add up.*

Her mind began to run wild. She shuddered at the thought of what her husband may have been doing in secret. Trust was on the line, and so was their marriage. Ashley knew the painful steps she had to take. Mark's problem was getting worse.

"Honey, let's talk. . . ."

❧

It's hard to admit, but we're all a little like Mark. Temptation hits and a tug-of-war between right and wrong is waged in our hearts. One voice screams, "Don't think—*just do it*!" Another whispers convicting words of truth and reason.

Whether we're entangled in a soul-robbing addiction or we suffer from a lying tongue, all sin grows the same way: "When tempted, no one should say, 'God is tempting me.' For God cannot be tempted by evil, nor does he tempt anyone; but each person is tempted when they are dragged away by their own evil desire and enticed. Then, after desire has conceived, it gives birth to sin; and sin, when it is full-grown, gives birth to death" (James 1:13–15).

If we're smart, we'll go immediately to God in prayer—confessing our sin, restoring our relationship with Him, and receiving His healing touch. While unconfessed sin will not break our *union* with Jesus, it will break our *communion* with Him. So removing any barrier between us and Jesus is critical. Healthy communion with our Lord is vital to spiritual growth, and growth is every Christ-follower's most important goal. We're given a short time on earth to get to know God—learning how to depend on Him and not ourselves, learning how to be like Christ, learning how to love, learning how to overcome. . .learning how to *live* this new life He has given us.

Confession and repentance are key to spiritual transformation.

Coming clean with God restores healthy communion with Him. C. S. Lewis explained it this way:

> *Christianity tells people to repent and promises them forgiveness. It therefore has nothing (as far as I know) to say to people who do not know that they have anything to repent of and who do not feel that they need forgiveness. It is after you have realized that there is a real Moral Law, and a Power behind that law, and that you have broken that law and put yourself wrong with that Power— it is after all this, and not a moment sooner, that Christianity begins to talk.[2]*

Confession is a crucial step we must take.

How Confession Works

Whether you're alone or with a friend, we recommend you confess your sin in prayer. As you humble yourself before the Father and engage in an honest conversation with the Son, you'll invite the Holy Spirit to minister to you—cleansing and healing you.

Essentially, confession means that we stand guilty before God's perfect justice. There's no place for pride or a self-righteous spirit as we enter into prayer. The life-giving intimacy we need can only be restored with a contrite heart, an acknowledgment of the wrong we've committed, and a sincere desire to repent. The apostle John wrote, "If we confess our sins, he is faithful and just and will forgive us our sins and purify us from all unrighteousness" (1 John 1:9).

The way we confess in prayer is up to us: We can pray while walking or driving, spontaneously, at home, at church, or at work. There is no ritual we have to follow or a specific posture of prayer. However, confession is a serious matter, so be sure you mean what you pray; God examines our hearts. I (Michael) prefer to be unhurried and in a quiet place so I can block out all distractions and give Jesus my full attention. And I believe that a heartfelt conversation is the best way to confess. While it's meaningful to end your time with God by reading a prayer of confession—for example, a psalm or other scripture passage—make sure you identify specific sins you have committed and confess them to Jesus in your own words.

Here's how I pray:

Dear Jesus, I come before You to confess my sin.
Lord, I agree that I am a sinner and that I have sinned.

Here's the sin I've committed: _____
[identify specific sin].
I'm sorry for sinning in this way,
and I ask for Your forgiveness.
Thank You, Jesus, for going to the cross
and forgiving this sin and all of my sins.
Lord, I love You, and I want to repent.
Please fill me with Your Holy Spirit and cleanse me.
Please protect me from the enemy.
Give me the strength to resist temptation.
And, Lord, please bring healing into my life.
Heal my heart. Heal my mind. Heal my motives
Heal my actions.
In Jesus' name I pray. Amen.

The Four Steps of Confession

1. *Admit the sin.* Admitting our sin is the healing answer to crippled faith and the way to bring our struggles into God's light. We don't have to live with a huge load of guilt and shame in our lives. Christ is reaching out to us with open arms—so we must go to Him in prayer and confess our sin.

   Putting a specific sin into words is necessary because of the power that comes when we drag the darkness into the light. "Everything exposed by the light becomes visible—and everything that is illuminated becomes a light" (Ephesians 5:13). As we engage in a prayer of confession, it's important that we identify the wrong we committed and bring every detail into Christ's cleansing light.

2. *Grieve your actions and tell God you're sorry.* This step is essential to restoring our relationship with Jesus and moving toward repentance. And there's a lot to grieve: the pain and loss that sin has caused, the pain we've caused others, the embarrassment, the wasted time and broken trust. We must take seriously the damage caused by sin, and we must especially grieve God's pain. Our Lord is saddened by the pain of sin and the pain of separation from him that the sin has caused. Don't cut this step short or try to minimize your feelings because they're uncomfortable. Grieving is an important step in the healing process.

3. *Ask God to forgive you and cleanse you.* God has promised forgiveness, but ask anyway. Jesus died for our sins, but ask anyway. And if your sin is against another person and you have confessed your sin to that person (see below), ask to be forgiven. It helps complete the circle for both you and that person and is the final step of removing the burden of sin from your mind and heart.

4. *Tell God you want to repent and follow Him.* Once you've confessed the sin and acknowledged Christ's forgiveness, it's time to make a complete 180-degree turn from the sin—called repentance. At this point, we can stop flogging ourselves. We're completely forgiven. Now with our relationship with God fully restored, we can take steps toward growth and change. (The Holy Spirit will help us.) Even if it's not the first time we've confessed this particular sin, God forgives us—again and again. Despite falling down, we gain strength each time we get up. Is this an excuse to sin, knowing we can confess it

and start over? Not at all! Some sins have such a grip on us that we may need to address them repeatedly.

∾

From the first page of the Bible to the very last, believers are challenged to overcome sin, counting ourselves dead to it and alive in Christ. "Therefore do not let sin reign in your mortal body so that you obey its evil desires. Do not offer any part of yourself to sin as an instrument of wickedness, but rather offer yourselves to God as those who have been brought from death to life; and offer every part of yourself to him as an instrument of righteousness. For sin shall no longer be your master, because you are not under the law, but under grace" (Romans 6:12–14).

A Prayer Warrior's Battle Plan

Sin gives Satan the upper hand in our lives. It erects a barrier between God and us; it creates strongholds that can be hard to break free from; it gives the enemy access to our lives, our minds, our hearts. Satan's influence can range from harassment through oppression and affliction all the way to bondage. And we can be in bondage to a wide variety of things: sexual addiction, alcohol, anger, worry, pride.

Temptation and sin are always accompanied by deceit. In other words, we can do bad things yet convince ourselves we are doing nothing wrong. According to author Patrick Means, an expert on addiction recovery, "When we want something badly enough, we'll deceive whomever we have to in order to get it. And the first person we have to deceive is ourselves." Means says we accomplish the self-deceit by telling ourselves two lies: (1) I don't really have a problem, and (2) I can handle this alone.[3]

We've given you this "prayer warrior's battle plan" to help you build the spiritual muscle to resist temptation and sin. Answer the following questions and take to heart the advice we've provided here.

List three examples of when you've told yourself a lie. Next, directly across from each lie, list a way you could have broken the self-deception cycle.

Lie:	Truth Step:
Lie:	Truth Step:
Lie:	Truth Step:

There are two types of people in the world: those whose problems are visible to everyone around them and those who attempt to carry around secrets. Sadly, far too many Christ-followers try to live in the second category, which ultimately puts them in the first category—usually at a cost: broken trust, ruined credibility, labels like "hypocrite."

What secrets are you keeping?

In what ways are they destructive?

Create a plan for giving them up:

Be warned: Avoid false repentance. Some people shed tears of sorrow, promising God they'll never again commit a certain sin. Then, a few days, weeks, or months later—when temptation builds to a fever pitch—they find themselves falling back into the same sin again. "When it comes to giving up a secret life," Means says,

"I believe there is a simple test to help us know whether we're experiencing true or false repentance. If I'm willing to tell someone else what I'm struggling with and ask for help, then it's true repentance. If I'm not willing to tell anyone else, I'm only fooling myself."[4]

Understand the battle that's being waged in your mind. *I'm hopeless—too far gone—and simply cannot change. I am what I am and will always be this way.* Ever catch yourself thinking these thoughts? If so, you've bought a lie whispered into your heart by the evil one. You're also trapped in a toxic shame cycle: You desperately want to change, yet you feel so flawed as an individual, you've concluded that you're "too far gone." So you buy Satan's lie that you're beyond God's help—continuing the cycle and prolonging the battle.

The truth is, there's a big difference between toxic shame and guilt. Guilt has to do with our behavior, what we do; shame has to do with our identity, who we are. Patrick Means explains it this way in his book *Men's Secret Wars*:

> *When we do something wrong, our God-given conscience rings an alarm. That pang we feel is guilt. Guilt is not destructive to our person because we can do something about it. We can acknowledge our wrongdoing, change our behavior, experience forgiveness, and we no longer have to feel guilty. . . . [Shame] pools and swirls outside the fringes of our lives like a poisonous nerve gas, waiting for us to open the door a crack and let it seep in to paralyze and destroy. Shame, in this sense, is a*

*demotivator for ongoing growth. It usually results
in self-condemnation, discouragement, and the urge
to give up.*[5]

Toxic shame eats away at our core: *There isn't an ounce of good left
in me. I'm so twisted and so bad, I simply cannot change. I'm hopeless,
worthless, and rejected. God will never accept me.*

According to Christian counselor Robert S. McGee, toxic
shame causes us to expect the worst from ourselves because we
believe that's who we are inside. "We're not surprised when we
disappoint people because deep down inside we know we're no
good."[6]

List three steps you will take to free yourself from toxic shame:
1.
2.
3.

Fight the enemy's lies. Believe that Jesus Christ loves you and
accepts you, despite your sin. Bestselling author Max Lucado has a
simple strategy for trusting God. In his book *He Still Moves Stones,*
Lucado writes: "Take Jesus at His word. Learn that when He says
something, it happens. When He says we're forgiven, let's unload
the guilt [and shame]. When He says we're valuable, let's believe
Him. When He says we're provided for, let's stop worrying."[7]

List three ways you will begin taking Jesus at His word:
1.
2.
3.

Read John 5:39–40. The Jewish priests in this passage—men who had committed their lives to studying Scriptures and to seeking God's Son—met Jesus face-to-face and yet rejected Him. Imagine that! They distrusted the Messiah because He didn't fit their human definition of how the Ultimate Role Model should look and behave.

Read the following scriptures and jot down your impressions of Jesus.

- John 15:13–17

- Matthew 9:35–36

- Colossians 1:13–20

- Revelation 3:20–22

- John 1:32–36

If Jesus is truly everything you just described, isn't it time to start trusting Him. . .and to get your faith growing again?

Write a prayer to Jesus expressing this desire.

Write your definition of "true Christianity":

Read Philippians 2:8; then read Romans 6:9–11.
- In what way do we also "die"?
- What responsibility do we have in our "deaths"? (Read Romans 6:11–14 for a giant hint.)

As you strive to be healed and made whole, wait patiently for the Lord. "God is never in a hurry," Lucado points out. He continues:

> *Then when He speaks to you—as He will—do what He tells you. It generally comes through your own conscience—a sort of growing conviction that such and such a course of action is the one He wants you to take. Or it may be given you in the advice of friends of sound judgment—those you love the most. God speaks sometimes through our circumstances and guides us, closing doors as well as opening them. He will let you know what you must do, and what you must be. He is waiting for you to touch Him (see Mark 5:31). The hand of faith is enough. Your trembling fingers can reach Him as He passes. Reach out your faith—touch Him. He will not ask, "Who touched me?" He will know.[8]*

5

THE SECRET OF VICTORIOUS LIVING

"All who are victorious will inherit all these blessings,
and I will be their God, and they will be my children."
REVELATION 21:7 NLT

John, now a seasoned "fisher of men"—wise in his years and a bit
slower in his step—took a deep breath of sea air and surveyed the
jagged coastline of Patmos.

A cloudless sky blended perfectly with the intense blue of
the Aegean, making it hard to tell where heaven ended and the
sea began. And just off to the east he spotted some hills on the
Asian mainland. John closed his eyes and groaned.

Despite all the beauty around him, this tiny Mediterranean
paradise was nothing more than a prison—a Roman penal colony
for those deemed political and religious troublemakers. And
that's exactly how the empire had labeled John.

It was AD 95, and a deluded emperor named Domitian
insisted that everyone address him as *dominus et deus* ("master
and god").[1] He simply wouldn't tolerate a scruffy band of radicals
who went around saying, "Jesus is Lord!" Those who challenged
him ended up destitute, dead. . .or detained.

By this time, John was the last living man who had been
intimate friends with Jesus. He'd given up everything to follow
the Lord—his family and friends, his home by the Sea of Galilee,
his father's lucrative fishing business. He was even willing to lay
down his life for the cause of Christ. Yet here he was, sitting on
a rock in the middle of the sea, cut off from the churches in his

care. . .blocked from doing the Lord's work.

Has it all been worth it?

Is God really in control of earthly events?

Can He change a sinful human heart?

The Roman army had leveled Jerusalem and burned its temple to the ground in an effort to stamp out a Jewish revolt.[2] And now, self-proclaimed "teachers of divine truth"—false prophets and ferocious wolves in sheep's clothing[3]—were confusing believers with a hodgepodge of spiritual teachings: a pinch of Plato, a dash of Persian dualism, one's ancestral cult for tradition's sake. . .and a little bit of Jesus thrown into the batch.[4] Countless Christians were falling for this stuff.

How can this be?

The war was won on the cross, so why is it still so hard to find the "narrow way"?

Why does it feel as if sin is getting the upper hand?

John was about to learn a key lesson: Two kingdoms had collided when Jesus hung from a cross. And believers are, in fact, on the winning side!

It was Sunday, and John took shelter in a hillside cave—his temporary home on Patmos (what many today call the Cave of the Apocalypse). As he began to pray and worship God, he was startled by a loud voice behind him, something like a piercing trumpet: "Write on a scroll what you see" (Revelation 1:11).

John turned around and was stunned. It was Jesus—but not just the man he broke bread with on the shores of the Tiberias, the One who showed him the holes in His hands and the side of His body.

The resurrected Lord stood before him, in wondrous glory, unveiled to John's mortal eyes, glowing with divine fire. This Jesus was a shocking vision of power and judgment and awe: He was positioned at the center of a gold menorah with seven branches, and He was dressed in a long robe with a golden sash around His chest. His head and hair were as white as snow, and His eyes were a flame of fire. His feet were like bronze glowing in a furnace, and His voice was like the sound of rushing waters. In His right hand He held seven stars, and out of His mouth came a sharp double-edged sword. His face shone like the sun.

It was simply too much for John to bear. He fainted dead at Christ's feet!

But then Jesus placed his right hand on the apostle and said: "Don't fear: I am First, I am Last, I'm Alive. I died, but I came to life, and my life is now forever. See these keys in my hand? They open and lock death's doors, they open and lock Hell's gates. Now write down everything you see: things that are, things about to be" (see Revelation 1:17–19 MSG).

Jesus opened John's mind to the spiritual realm, giving him a personal tour of heaven and what had to happen before anyone could get there. Unimaginable visions began to flash before his eyes—scene after scene of doom and deliverance, terror and triumph. . .a rush of color and sound, image and energy.

Each one shouted a single message: "Yes, I am still in control."

John learned that things were not as they seemed. Evil, though widespread, was not winning. Faithfulness, though costly, was not futile. Affliction, though continuing, would most definitely end. "The Lion's roar will soon be heard. Until then, we must reign with the Lamb."[5]

And seven times, Jesus revealed the secret to finding the path home, the "narrow way." Jesus calls us to overcome, to conquer—to be *victorious* in Him!

Revelation 2:7 NLT: "Anyone with ears to hear must listen to the Spirit and understand what he is saying to the churches. To everyone who is victorious I will give fruit from the tree of life in the paradise of God."

Revelation 2:11 NLT: "Anyone with ears to hear must listen to the Spirit and understand what he is saying to the churches. Whoever is victorious will not be harmed by the second death."

Revelation 2:17 NLT: "Anyone with ears to hear must listen to the Spirit and understand what he is saying to the churches. To everyone who is victorious I will give some of the manna that has been hidden away in heaven. And I will give to each one a white stone, and on the stone will be engraved a new name that no one understands except the one who receives it."

Revelation 2:26–29 NLT: "To all who are victorious, who obey me to the very end, to them I will give authority over all the nations. They will rule the nations with an iron rod and smash them like clay pots. They will have the same authority I received from my Father, and I will also give them the morning star! Anyone with ears to hear must listen to the Spirit and understand what he is saying to the churches."

Revelation 3:5 NLT: "All who are victorious will be clothed in white. I will never erase their names from the Book of Life, but I will announce before my Father and his angels that they are mine."

Revelation 3:12 NLT: "All who are victorious will become pillars in the Temple of my God, and they will never have to leave it. And I will write on them the name of my God, and they will be citizens in the city of my God—the new Jerusalem that comes down from heaven from my God. And I will also write on them my new name."

Revelation 3:21 NLT: "Those who are victorious will sit with me on my throne, just as I was victorious and sat with my Father on his throne."

Revelation 21:7 NLT: "All who are victorious will inherit all these blessings, and I will be their God, and they will be my children."

A Powerful Plan for Spiritual Growth

Fast-forward a couple thousand years into the future.

Jesus is still very much in control, but at times it's easy to feel John's frustration as he sat on a tiny island in the middle of the sea. At times we all feel isolated, stuck, powerless. People are still just as selfish and mixed up as they were in John's day, and countless believers are still falling for a hodgepodge of spiritual teachings with a little bit of Jesus thrown into the batch.

Yet Christ's words are crystal clear: *overcome, conquer, be victorious.* The question is. . .how?

Answer: A powerful combination—daily, persistent, fervent *prayer* mixed with *Bible engagement* and the strength of the *Holy Spirit.* In Matthew 4:1–11—the account of Christ's temptation in the wilderness—we get a clear picture of how this combination can protect us against the schemes of the Enemy.

Jesus was led by the Spirit into the wilderness to be tempted by the devil. And after fasting forty days and forty nights, Jesus was hungry. He decided to rest in a shady spot, the shadow of a boulder. His eyes were closed and He was leaning against the giant stone. Suddenly, He sensed an icy presence, the presence of evil.

The Lord raised His head and squinted. A few feet away, a flash of white light rose from the desert into the sky, the radiance of supernatural power. Slowly coming into focus within the center of this light was the image of a handsome man. The light was this curious figure.

With an arrogant yet almost sympathetic tone, the light spoke. "Since You are God's Son, speak the word that will turn these stones into loaves of bread."[6]

At first, Jesus neither stood nor answered. He regarded the light as though it were a savage beast sniffing too close to Him. Then He closed His eyes again and in a hoarse voice whispered, "It is written, 'No one lives by bread alone, but by every word that issues from the mouth of God.' "

All at once, the cold presence completely engulfed Jesus. A wind arose and began to howl. When the Lord opened His eyes, He found that the light had completely surrounded Him, canceling the desert in a pale fog. Then He felt a footing beneath Him. He stood, and the light released Him, moving to one side so that Jesus was able to see that He had been transported to the highest corner of the temple wall. Scattered like pebbles below Him was the Holy City, Jerusalem. "Here the priests blew trumpets to usher in the New Year. Here the air was thin and the height was giddy."[7]

The icy light spoke again. "Jump, and prove You are the Son of God." The presence goaded Him, quoting Psalm 91: "For the Scriptures declare, 'God will send His angels to keep You from harm'—they will prevent You from smashing on the rocks below."[8]

Jesus countered with a citation from Deuteronomy: "Scripture also says not to put the Lord your God to a foolish test!"

In a flash, the Holy City vanished, and Jesus was no longer on the temple wall. He was now infinitely higher than anything made by human hands. Standing on a cosmic mountain, the presence gestured expansively—pointing out all the earth's kingdoms and their glorious splendor. Then he said, "They're Yours—lock, stock, and barrel. Just fall down on Your knees and worship me, and they're Yours."

But Jesus did not look at the kingdoms of the world, and His refusal was stern: "I know you. I know what sort of angel you are. Satan, tempter, betrayer—get out of here!" The Savior backed His rebuke with another quotation from Deuteronomy: "Worship the Lord your God, and only Him. Serve Him with absolute single-heartedness."

In an instant, Jesus was sitting in the desert again, leaning against a boulder. The test was over and the devil was gone. In place of the icy presence were warmth and peace and goodness. Angels came down from heaven to care for the Savior.[9]

Even though He was physically exhausted, Jesus won. He had powerful ammunition: the work of the Holy Spirit, the Word of God, and an active prayer life.

Let's explore some practical ways this spiritual arsenal can help us.

The Secret of Victorious Living: The Holy Spirit

The moment you accepted Christ as your Lord and Savior, the Holy Spirit took up residence in your heart. "Do you not know that your bodies are temples of the Holy Spirit, who is in you, whom you have received from God? You are not your own" (1 Corinthians 6:19). The Holy Spirit is the most powerful Being in the world today. Old Testament times were the age of God the Father, and when Jesus walked the earth, it was the time of God the Son. Since Pentecost, we have been living in the age of God the Holy Spirit.

The Reverend Billy Graham says the Holy Spirit is the

Source of victorious living for every Christ-follower:

> *It is only the consecrated, Spirit-filled Christian*
> *who can have victory of the world, the flesh, and*
> *the Devil. It is the Holy Spirit who will do the*
> *fighting for you. "We wrestle not against flesh and*
> *blood, but against principalities, against powers,*
> *against the rulers of darkness" (Ephesians 6:12).*
> *This is a spiritual warfare. You cannot fight against*
> *these three enemies with normal weapons. Only as*
> *we become channels and let the Holy Spirit do the*
> *fighting through us are we going to get complete*
> *victory. Don't hold back anything from Christ. Let*
> *Him be completely the Lord and Master of your life.*
> *He said, "Ye call me Master and Lord: and ye say*
> *well; for so I am" (John 13:13).[10]*

The Secret of Victorious Living: Bible Engagement

At Back to the Bible, we love to shock people a bit by telling them, "Stop reading your Bible." We quickly follow that statement with the key to finding victory in Christ: "Start engaging your Bible."

Here's how we define Bible engagement: *We receive, reflect on, and respond to God's Word consistently.*

Let's focus on the middle part of our definition: *reflect.*

To tap into the power of God's Word, we actively meditate on, pray about, and ponder the words of the Bible. Not only is reflection (or meditation) an active consideration of biblical truth, but it is also commanded by God. Romans 12:2 tells us, "Be transformed by the renewing of your mind. Then you will be able to test and approve what God's will is—his good, pleasing and perfect will."

Reflection fosters understanding, and understanding enables us to hear God's personal message to each one of us. Let us demonstrate what we mean with an example. Take a close look at Christ's words in Luke 6:46–49:

> *"Why do you call me, 'Lord, Lord,' and do not do what I say? As for everyone who comes to me and hears my words and puts them into practice, I will show you what they are like. They are like a man building a house, who dug down deep and laid the foundation on rock. When a flood came, the torrent struck that house but could not shake it, because it was well built. But the one who hears my words and does not put them into practice is like a man who built a house on the ground without a foundation. The moment the torrent struck that house, it collapsed and its destruction was complete."*

Got it? Now go back and read the passage a couple more times, *meditating* on what Jesus is saying here. Pull it apart sentence by sentence and *listen* to His voice, His heart. Allow the Holy Spirit to speak to you.

Ponder His words on an intellectual level: What is Jesus saying through these verses? What's a key message here? Is there a warning or a promise? Is He teaching me about God's character or my eternal destiny?

Ponder His words on a relational level: How do these verses apply uniquely to me? Is Jesus calling me to action? Is He telling me to slow down and listen more? Is He encouraging me or disciplining me? Have I been neglecting Him or others?

Then get more personal:

"Here's how I feel about these verses. . ."

"Here's what's hard, God. . ."

"Help me understand, because I don't get this. . ."

"Help me move from this way of thinking to what You want. . ."

Finally, pray through the passage: "Lord, what do You want me to do with these words?"

∾

Through the process of Bible engagement, we reap two great benefits in our lives:

1. We enable God's Word to shape our thinking and sharpen our ability to understand His will. Daniel (see Daniel 7:28) and Mary (see Luke 2:19, 51) offer prime examples of why reflection on God's Word is essential to spiritual growth. Each of them faced situations in which they couldn't figure out what God was doing in their lives. Yet instead of giving up, they both did their best to carefully ponder their situations. Their actions remind us to submit to God's greater wisdom, even when His work doesn't make much sense to us.

2. We saturate our minds with Scripture—which can help us to battle temptation and sin. Engaging with the Bible won't make us perfect, but it will help us to think the way God thinks. And that will help us to obey Him and do His will. Our obedience will eventually turn into desire.

Biblical meditation is actually the thoughtful contemplation of God's Word, as well as reflection on God and the person and work of Jesus Christ. It is a powerful tool when used with prayer and Bible reading. It's doesn't have to be—as some Eastern religions teach—an emptying of our minds for the purposes of relaxation or other self-serving results. What we're talking about involves serious effort, because pondering God's Word requires focus—intense mental activity coupled with emotional energy. And it's worth it.

∽

The secret to victorious living is in our grasp.

Life with Christ is an amazing adventure, and we won't want to miss a second of it. The late Christian artist Rich Mullins sums it up best: "The goal is not that you should become a great Bible scholar. It's not about mere intellectual assent to a set of doctrines. The goal is that you should be like Jesus—and scripture can help you with that. I don't need to read the Bible because I'm a great saint. I read the Bible because I'll find God there. It's about a daily walk with this person Jesus.[11]

6

FIFTY FACTS ABOUT PRAYER, THE BIBLE, FAITH, AND SPIRITUAL GROWTH

Don't worry about anything; instead, pray about everything. Tell God
what you need, and thank him for all he has done. Then you will
experience God's peace, which exceeds anything we can understand.
His peace will guard your hearts and minds as you live in Christ Jesus.

PHILIPPIANS 4:6–7 NLT

Since 2003, the Center for Bible Engagement (CBE) at Back to the Bible has studied the spiritual lives of believers around the world—so far more than 170,000 in twenty-two countries. Our research has focused primarily on how people grow spiritually, how they engage (or don't engage) the Bible, and what temptations they encounter each day. Here are several highlights from our study, along with findings from other reliable sources.

1. Scientists now have evidence that prayer and meditation can change our brains. According to neuroscientist Richard Davidson, studies of those who pray or meditate for one, two, or more hours a day show changes—improvements—in their brains. "You can sculpt your brain just as you'd sculpt your muscles if you went to the gym," he says. "Our brains are continuously being sculpted, whether you like it or not, wittingly or unwittingly."[1]

2. A doctor at a Philadelphia hospital says prayer is not a cure for cancer—but can sometimes be as important as science in helping patients heal. Dr. Andrew Newberg of Thomas Jefferson Hospital has been studying the effect of prayer on the human brain for more than twenty years, injecting radioactive dye into subjects and watching what changes inside their heads when they pray. "You can see it's all red here when the person is just at rest," said Newberg, pointing at a computer screen showing brain activity, "but you see it turns into these yellow colors when she's actually doing prayer."[2]

3. Mature believers have discovered that spiritual growth happens through (1) prayer, (2) meditation on God's Word, and (3) Bible engagement.

4. Spiritual maturity is genuine and evident in our lives when (1) we pray and engage scripture consistently and daily, (2) we put feet on our faith and live out the Word in loving obedience to Christ, and (3) we roll up our sleeves and share the Word by serving others and laying down our lives for Christ.

5. There are four critical elements of spiritual growth: (1) the *knowledge* element: we hear from God and reflect on His Word; (2) the *prayer* element: we prepare our heart through confession and pray in the Word; (3) the *faith* element: we believe God's Word, trust His direction, and internalize His message; and (4) the *action* element: we live out the Word, flourish in it, and grow spiritually.

6. The key to dealing with a multitude of struggles is prayer coupled with Bible reading. For example, when people wrestle with lust, they must use a "protective verse" (such as 1 Corinthians 6:18–20) as a shield and even repeat it in the face of temptation: "Flee from sexual immorality. . . . You are not your own; you were bought at a price. Therefore honor God with your bodies."

7. Christians grow through *relationship*, not *religion*.

8. Relationship with God is two-way.

9. We must *engage* the Bible, not just read it.

10. Bible engagement is an essential way in which God communicates with Christ-followers.

11. Almost half of the North American Christians we surveyed did not read or engage the Bible daily.

12. Almost half of North American Christians in our survey did not know (1) what the Bible is or (2) what the Bible is for.

13. Disengagement from the Bible leaves American believers ignorant of basic scriptural truths, vulnerable to false teachings, spiritually immature, and reflecting on a "fantasy-based" image of their Creator instead of the one true God of the Bible.

14. Many believers don't grasp that through the Word, God teaches, rebukes, corrects, and trains us in righteousness.

15. Without the Bible, we wouldn't know (1) what God is like, (2) what His plan is for us, (3) how much He loves us, (4) the right way to live, or (5) anything about what will happen to us after we die.

16. Bible engagement four or more times per week changes behavior.

17. Those who have four or more "scriptural touches" (encounters with scripture) per week described the "feelings" they received after prayer and Bible reading as "impressions from the Holy Spirit." Question: Does increased Bible engagement allow believers to tune in promptings from the Holy Spirit more clearly and more frequently?

18. There were no significant differences in behaviors and spiritual growth when CBE compared church attendance to Bible reading. Therefore, we concluded that scripture engagement is a more accurate measure of spiritual growth than church attendance.

19. There are two types of Christians: *notional Christ-followers* (those who believe in "their concept" of Christ and interact with Him in a one-way relationship) and *relational Christ-followers* (those who have a two-way relationship with the true Christ of the Bible).

20. God wants us to move from being a notional Christ-follower to being a relational Christ-follower.

21. Observable characteristics of relational Christ-followers:
    - Pray consistently
    - Engage scripture four or more times per week
    - Hear from God through (1) the Bible, (2) impressions prompted by the Holy Spirit, and (3) other people
    - Demonstrate moderate to extensive Bible knowledge
    - Memorize verses
    - Have read the entire Bible at least once
    - Are passionate about connecting with God
    - Share their faith with others
    - Are less likely to take part in negative and immoral behaviors, specifically viewing pornography, gambling, abusing illegal drugs, pursuing drunkenness, and engaging in sex outside of marriage

22. Observable characteristics of notional Christ followers:
    - Occasionally engage scripture (zero to three times per week)
        → Those who engage scripture three or more times per week hear from God through (1) feelings, (2) the Bible, and (3) people.
        → Those who rarely engage scripture or who do so once a week hear from God through (1) people, (2) feelings, and (3) the Bible.
    - Demonstrate little Bible knowledge

- Rarely pray or memorize verses
- Are less likely to have read the entire Bible
- Are less likely to share their faith with others
- Are more likely to take part in negative and immoral behaviors, specifically viewing pornography, gambling, abusing illegal drugs, pursuing drunkenness, and engaging in sex outside of marriage

23. Those who are notional Christ followers have not genuinely become new creations in Christ, do not exhibit a change in their lifestyles, and often revert to past sins and struggles.

24. Those who are notional Christ followers live with a belief system grounded on a "fantasy-based" image of their Creator. Instead of connecting with the one true God of the Bible, notional believers fit the Lord into who they believe He is (or want Him to be).

25. Very often, the notional Christ follower does not engage in scripture since the Bible is not relevant to his or her fantasy-based notion of Christ.

26. Relational Christ-followers are more in tune with God. They have discovered their unique "spiritual rhythms"— ways of connecting with God and growing deeper in their relationship with Him.

27. Relational Christ-followers are often more in tune with the needs of others.

28. Christians often don't agree on the definition of the word *spiritual.*

29. Many Christians don't know how to grow spiritually.

30. Despite differences of opinion about what is and isn't spiritual, everyone—Christians and nonbelievers alike—wants to win the day spiritually. Most don't know how to accomplish this (or where to begin).

31. An ongoing study at CBE is revealing that emotional well-being, hope, and the fruit of the Spirit (as outlined in Galatians 5:22–23) grow when individuals engage the Holy Bible, but not when they read and internalize other religious works such as the Qur'an or the Book of Mormon.

32. Temptation can be defeated through Bible engagement.

33. Four out of five survey respondents reported being tempted between one and ten times a day.

34. Seventy-nine percent of survey respondents admitted that they yield to their temptations "at least some of the time."

35. Not surprisingly, men and women struggle with different kinds of temptations.

36. For women, gossip and overeating ranked as their biggest struggles.

37. For men, sexually related issues ranked as their biggest struggles.

38. Giving in to temptation and sinning cripples a believer's witness and is a hindrance to spiritual growth.

39. Sin does not happen in a vacuum. One person's sin affects others.

40. Spiritual growth does not happen in a vacuum. One person's spiritual victory affects others.

41. Getting unstuck from struggles—overcoming temptation, bad habits, and sinful behaviors—involves a change in the way we think. The "Philippians 4:8 principle" is a place to start: Meditate on those things that are true, noble, right, pure, lovely, admirable, excellent, and praiseworthy.

42. Running toward God is the solution to winning the day spiritually, especially when we face seemingly insurmountable challenges in our lives.

43. Regarding lasting spiritual growth, the mere transference of content (faith-building books and other resources, for example) isn't the key. In fact, content is often quickly forgotten.

44. Training Christ-followers in a *process* of spiritual growth is most effective. Such a process involves a methodology built around where the individual is spiritually and continues until the believer engages the Bible on a daily basis.

45. Teaching someone the "how" and "why" versus only the "what" makes a huge difference in their spiritual development. Therefore, church leaders, Christian ministries, and spiritual growth resources should teach believers both (1) how to engage God and His Word and (2) how to engage God *through* His Word.

46. A Bible-engagement discipleship program equips believers to continually engage and communicate with God even if the leader (a pastor, a teacher, an author) is no longer around. CBE has developed state-of-the-art "touches" (biblically based resources and social media programs) that can help believers grow spiritually.

47. We fail spiritually when we (1) don't engage God, (2) don't engage scripture, (3) stay in a notional relationship, (4) follow impersonal "religious practices" instead of engaging in a relationship with God, and (5) get stuck in (and comfortable with) wrong thinking and sinful behaviors.

48. We can recover from sin and self-defeating behaviors— and ultimately have success spiritually—if we learn how to "crawl, walk, and run" when we face a battle. In other

words, we respond differently depending on the struggle and the season of our faith. (Sometimes we behave like a mature believer and walk steadfastly or run; at other moments we must respond like a new believer and crawl.)

49. It's no secret: life, faith, and spiritual growth are often messy and unpredictable. The truth is, we don't mature and move toward God in a sequential or linear fashion. Spiritual growth moves in multiple directions (toward self and toward Christ) all at once. Understanding this truth is a key to spiritual success.

50. Those around us will notice as we attempt to live our lives with an honest and real connection with God.

Part Three

PRAYERS FOR
ALL OCCASIONS

7

SIX BASIC TYPES OF PRAYER

"I tell you, you can pray for anything, and if
you believe that you've received it, it will be yours."
MARK 11:24 NLT

The concept of prayer seems fairly basic on the surface. But it is as individual as each human being. Yes, prayer is an amazing tool God has offered us. It is available to every person who walks the earth. But it also takes on different shapes and sizes as we interact with God in our own way. Direct communication with our Creator is as dynamic and personal as our relationship with God. We seek as God directs. We confess as God convicts. We trust as God loves.

I (Tiffany) remember one of my earliest childhood memories of prayer. We attended a small country church where it wasn't uncommon to hear "Amen!" and "Preach it!" during the service. The preacher was usually excited and we had no problem hearing him as he spoke. And when it was time for prayer, it was common for the entire church to gather around the altar and pray together. People would kneel, stand, or sit on the front pew in close proximity to one another. When the prayer began, everyone spoke out loud. It wasn't weird or crazy. Most spoke in a soft voice as they reached out to God. Some would smile and raise their hands while others held tightly to the altar as they cried. This portion of the service usually lasted about ten to fifteen minutes. As the prayers concluded, folks would find their way back to their seats and the service would continue.

As a child, I thought all churches prayed this way. So I was really confused when a friend of mine said she never prayed because she couldn't remember her prayers. I had no idea what she was talking about. Memorized prayers were a foreign concept to me. With further conversation, I realized that her church had a set of prayers they would pray together and/or privately. I was fascinated by this idea. As an adult I began to look into this idea more closely and came to realize that many churches throughout the world have this tradition. And as I read their prayers, I saw they were well written, inspirational, and brimming with theological meaning. There were many different kinds of prayers, including praise, petition, confession, and thanksgiving. They were prayers just like mine, but written down and memorized. There was no rule that only these prayers could be spoken. They were just a starting point to offer a framework for a believer's prayer life.

The wisdom contained in written prayers can be insightful and profound. These prayers can be a great way to learn more about God. And someone praying these prayers can do so earnestly and honestly. But prayer is so much more than that. It is a live conversation that cannot be scripted. Begin with a memorized prayer if you choose. The goal is to place ourselves in the presence of God. As we enter into that special place, the Spirit will guide us in what to say and how to listen. These are moments that shape us into God's people by enabling us to connect with the Source of love and forgiveness. The framework is only there to help us get started. Let's explore some of the most common types of prayers.

1. Prayer of Intercession: Acting on Behalf of Others

For this reason, ever since I heard about your
faith in the Lord Jesus and your love for all God's
people, I have not stopped giving thanks for you,
remembering you in my prayers. I keep asking that
the God of our Lord Jesus Christ, the glorious Father,
may give you the Spirit of wisdom and revelation, so
that you may know him better. I pray that the eyes of
your heart may be enlightened in order that you may
know the hope to which he has called you, the riches
of his glorious inheritance in his holy people, and his
incomparably great power for us who believe.

Ephesians 1:15–19

Intercessory prayer can be specific—focused on intimate details of a person's life—or it may be general: praying for a nation or a community. The Bible contains many examples of intercessory prayer. Cries for a nation's welfare, prayers for protection of troops during battle, petitions for healing, pleas for relief from the torment of evil spirits, and requests for salvation are found throughout both the Old and New Testaments. The passage above is an example of Paul interceding for the church at Ephesus. He prayed for God's blessing on the people who worshipped there.

Intercession means praying on behalf of someone else. There are so many situations in which this type of prayer is needed. It is a powerful way to seek God's provision and direction on behalf of others. Perhaps someone is unconscious—someone who has been in an accident and is undergoing surgery, for example. Maybe someone is facing troubled times and need prayer support. Our prayers could plead for protection and safety for foreign missionaries. Corporate prayers bring faith communities together as they focus on the needs of others. Or maybe someone close is spiritually lost and simply doesn't acknowledge God.

When we intercede for others, we draw close to Christ's heart—actually joining Him in prayer. In heaven, Jesus is our High Priest who intercedes with the Father for all of humankind.

2. Prayer of Consecration and Dedication: Launching Christ-followers

> *[Jesus] withdrew about a stone's throw beyond them,*
> *knelt down and prayed, "Father, if you are willing, take*
> *this cup from me; yet not my will, but yours be done."*
> LUKE 22:41–42

"Yet not my will, but yours be done." Wow, those are powerful words. They represent one of the hardest prayers to pray. A life of faith looks good on paper. The idea that God loves us and forgives our sins is amazing. We try to make good decisions and live our lives with integrity. But so often, life gets hard. Real everyday challenges are around every corner. With all the dynamics of interpersonal relationships, past experiences, moral dilemmas, and tough questions, we sometimes don't know which direction to go. Or even harder is when we feel led to a certain path that may be difficult to walk. This is when our prayer life gets real. As we communicate with our Creator, we may not like what we hear. For example, we may want to pray for revenge, but God is asking us to forgive. We may pray for financial gain, but God is leading us to simplify our lives. We may pray to get married to a certain person, but God has someone better for you down the road. Above all of the details, God desires for us to come to prayer with an attitude of reverence and humility.

Any honest conversation is going to be filled with ups and downs. Prayer is no different.

Jesus' prayer on the Mount of Olives is a perfect example of this type of prayer. During those tense moments before He was arrested—and ultimately led to the cross—the Lord committed Himself to God's will. It wasn't easy, but the Son of God was able to trust enough to say, "Yet not my will, but yours be done." What a great example for us! We have properly placed ourselves in the presence of God when we are able to trust in the midst of fear—because only the Spirit can bring such peace. Prayer is an amazing way to connect with the Source of our salvation. The same power that saves us will bring us through the tough times. But we must be willing to say, "Your will, not mine."

3. Prayer of Praise and Worship: Glorifying God

The shepherds returned, glorifying and praising
God for all the things they had heard and seen,
which were just as they had been told.
LUKE 2:20

Worship. This word can mean so many different things to different people. But the essence of worship is to praise our Creator. Sometimes our prayers may only focus on recognizing and remembering what God has done for us. Expressing our love and adoration for the Lord is one way of thanking our Creator for the many blessings in our lives. Shout, sing, clap, cry, laugh, jump, and dance before the Lord. Don't be afraid of showing your joyful emotion as you celebrate God.

The Bible is filled with many examples. Here are a few highlights:

Luke 11:2 (NKJV): In the Lord's Prayer, Jesus instructs His disciples to praise God: "When you pray, say: Our Father in heaven, hallowed be Your name. . ."

Luke 18:43 (NKJV): The man whom Jesus healed of blindness is described as "glorifying God." And all the people who witnessed the miracle "gave praise to God." They prayed prayers of thanksgiving.

John 11:41 (NKJV): As Jesus stands outside the tomb of Lazarus, moments before He raises His friend from the dead, He looks up and says, "Father, I thank You that You have heard Me."

4. Prayer of Faith: Our Petitions to God

"Therefore I tell you, whatever you ask for in prayer,
believe that you have received it, and it will be yours "
MARK 11:24

Bringing our needs and petitions before the Lord is a personal and intimate experience. These private conversations reach to the innermost corners of our lives as we reveal our need for the Savior. Such moments of honesty and vulnerability build our faith as we trust that God will lead us through any challenge. A prayer of faith can be expressed in a variety of ways; this kind of prayer represents our specific requests, our many petitions, and our countless hopes and desires that we ask the Lord to bless and to fulfill—if, of course, it is His will to do so.

The word *petition* means to ask for something. When our prayers are in line with God's will, we can be confident they will be answered. But we also must trust in God's timing. We must be prepared to wait. This is where our faith grows because we trust that God's will and timing are for our best. Read through the New Testament and explore the many times Jesus said the words "according to your faith." He could see into people's motives and intentions. He knew when they were truly seeking Him or simply seeking their own desires. For example, when Jesus went to His hometown of Nazareth, scripture says He "did not do many miracles there because of their lack of faith" (Matthew 13:58). He wants our hearts to be filled with a desire to know Him more. He recognizes our trust as we wait. It is our faith that brings us in alignment with God's will. And if we lack faith, we can always ask for more. These prayers draw us closer to the Lord just by asking for help to trust God more.

5. Prayer of Agreement: United in Cause

"Again, truly I tell you that if two of you on earth agree about anything they ask for, it will be done for them by my Father in heaven. For where two or three gather in my name, there am I with them."

MATTHEW 18:19–20

We were created to live in community with our Lord and with one another. Though we have all been created as unique individuals with different talents and abilities, we are all called to seek God. Indeed, a beautiful union takes place when God's people join together in a shared prayer. Our unity is rooted in our Creator. The common goal of growing in Christ is what brings such diversity together. As the Church grows in faith and understanding, we find common ground with one another as our desires become more and more focused on God's will.

When two people are in harmony with one another regarding a specific prayer request—essentially praying for the exact same thing—there is power in their unity, and the faith, passion, and commitment of these Christ-followers can move the hand of God.

While the Lord wants our daily one-on-one time with Him to be a priority, united group prayer also has an important place in believers' lives. For example, when my mother was involved in a head-on collision while driving on a windy mountain road, my family and friends quickly joined each other in prayer. We were most definitely in agreement, interceding for my mom's health, safety, and well-being. I've learned firsthand that fervent, focused prayers of agreement can result in miracles.

6. Prayer of Binding and Loosing: Praying in God's Authority

> *"Truly I tell you, whatever you bind on earth*
> *will be bound in heaven, and whatever you*
> *loose on earth will be loosed in heaven."*
> MATTHEW 18:18

Jesus tells us in this verse that we have authority in His name. But again, that authority is based on our desire for God's will to be done, not our own wishes. God's power flows through us when we seek Him first. We are joining the work of the Spirit that is already in motion. As we seek to align our thoughts and requests with the will of God, our desires are conformed to those of our Lord. In this way, we participate in God's mighty work of redemption. So a prayer of binding and loosing should never be entered into casually. It's serious business!

As we call upon the Lord, we must remember that He will display His power for His glory. God's salvation and forgiveness are for everyone; the Spirit moves on behalf of all humans. As we align our will with God's, we too will begin to have more compassion for others. So asking God to bind or loose His power in a particular situation must be in the best interest of others. We ask for a force to be bound out of a desire for protection, not as a method of revenge. We ask for God's power to be loosened for the benefit of others, not because of our own desire to brag or boast. But if we pray that God's will be done, then we get to be a part of something powerful and life changing. And being involved in God's work in this way shapes us as much as the person we are praying for.

Connect with Him

Throughout the years I have witnessed and experienced several types of prayer. I have come to embrace any prayer that enhances my connection with God. Sometimes my prayers are about personal concerns, while other times I intercede for friends or family. Sometimes they are focused on praising God, and other times they are an act of confession. As the Spirit leads, my prayers are shaped by the needs of the moment. They represent where I am in my walk with the Lord at that particular time. They aren't perfect or poetic, but they come from the heart. And that is what God desires.

8

LEARNING FROM THE LORD'S PRAYER

"This, then, is how you should pray: 'Our Father in heaven, hallowed be your name, your kingdom come, your will be done, on earth as it is in heaven. Give us today our daily bread. And forgive us our debts, as we also have forgiven our debtors. And lead us not into temptation, but deliver us from the evil one.' "

MATTHEW 6:9–13

Christ has given us the perfect prayer.

His words in Matthew 6:9–13—known as the Lord's Prayer—offer us an example of how we should pray because it mirrors God's will for His people.[1] It shows how Christians should live and provides the Jesus-breathed basics of what He wants us to focus on. When prayed diligently, with thoughtful reverence, it clears out the mistakes of yesterday and the worries of tomorrow and gets our mind off of the problems, cares, inadequacies, and failures of the day. As we take to heart these powerful words, the Lord transforms our desires, molding them more into what He'd rather they be—a yearning to follow the Great Commandment to love God and love others.

Yet this kind of spiritual growth certainly won't happen overnight—and may prove to be quite challenging for many of us. Why? It requires a 180-degree shift in our often "me-centered" mind-set. As Max Lucado observes, "One source of man's weariness is the pursuit of things that can never satisfy; but which one of us has not been caught up in that pursuit at some time in our life? Our passions, possessions and pride—these are all *dead* things. When we try to get life out of dead things, the result is only weariness and dissatisfaction."[2]

Ready to let go of empty pursuits and dead things? Ready to enjoy the satisfaction of knowing and living God's will? The Lord's Prayer can help. Let's pull it apart line by line to unlock its power. But before we begin, let us caution you: Don't misuse this remarkable prayer by praying it with the wrong motives or mechanically repeating the words—in other words, praying from your head and not your heart. These words must come from your heart, your mind, your *whole being*.

Pastor and bestselling author R.T. Kendall offers some clues:

> *What, then, is the point of the Lord's Prayer? Although it is a prayer to be prayed by all of us, it is a pattern prayer. For example, it begins with acknowledging God, worshiping Him and focusing on His interests. Then come the petitions that pertain to us. This pattern is designed to show that we are not to rush into the presence of God, snap our fingers toward heaven and expect the angels to jump! We begin with proper worship.*
>
> *All good praying should, in some way, be consistent with the pattern, order, content, and intent of the Lord's Prayer. It is a prayer to be prayed, but the words of the Lord's Prayer serve also as an outline of appropriate praying. We should see each line of the Lord's Prayer—that is, each petition—as the solid foundation for truly worshipful and selfless praying.[3]*

A Point to Ponder: Prayer is a miracle, and the sooner we realize this fact, the sooner prayer ceases to be a dull routine or a religious burden. According to author and radio Bible teacher Warren Wiersbe, "Prayer is an exciting adventure that molds our lives and the lives of those for whom we pray. If prayer is a neglected or ignored discipline in your life, then it's time you attempted to measure this miracle and discover what you are missing."[4]

Regaining the Wonder: "Our Father in heaven, hallowed be your name"

When we think of God, what images come to mind? An impersonal judge banging His gavel—sentencing us to "life without parole"? The unapproachable burning bush that Moses encountered? An impersonal spirit with no ability to affect our day?

If we peered into a telescope to study the heavens, we would no doubt conclude, as C. S. Lewis remarked, that our Creator is "quite merciless and no friend to man. . . . The universe is dangerous and terrifying."[5] Some conclude, then, that God is to be feared and is unapproachable. He's that mean Old Testament judge destroying whole people groups because of their bad behavior and wrong belief. Consequently, they try to keep out of His way as much as possible and never draw near to the God of the New Testament.

Who is this God—the only true God revealed in the Bible?

Hebrews 1:3 says that Jesus "is the radiance of God's glory and the exact representation of his being." Jesus said, "Anyone who has seen me has seen the Father" (John 14:9). What is God's character like? It's like Jesus. It's a forgiving father embracing his prodigal son. It's not the wonder of the heavens that the Old Testament mentions; it's the wonder of His love.

I (Arnie) have had to progress in my own understanding of the character of God. As a young man, I believed that I couldn't live the pure life in my actions, so I determined I wouldn't try. When I came to the end of myself and started to look deeper, I found that God isn't a God of debits and credits; rather, He unconditionally loves any who humbly admit their sin and genuinely realize they need a Savior.

There is a wonder and awe about the simplicity of God's love. Creation, yes; salvation, to be sure—both have their own depth of wonder. But the daily love and concern God has for His children is truly *awe*some.

> **A Point to Ponder:** It's important that we know the truth about Jesus. Wrong thoughts about our Lord can cripple our ability to succeed spiritually. After all, an idol of the mind is as dangerous as an idol of the hands. And many Christians have a variety of wrong idols when it comes to the character of God. Take some time today to explore the full picture of God. Strive to be attracted to Him with a new awe and wonder.

Living the Lord's Prayer

We invite you to take part in an exercise that will nurture personal application of the Lord's

Prayer. The goal is to help you pray these special words from the heart, not just recite them mechanically. At the end of each section, express to Jesus what each portion of the prayer means to you. For example, this section explores the line *"Our Father in heaven, hallowed be Your name."* Here's what I (Arnie) feel when I encounter these words:

O God my Father, I realize how holy and perfect You are. . .and how I am not. So love me and walk with me today amid my imperfection, and I will try to walk with You today amid Your perfect love. You're a good Father who loves me, Your child, no matter what the day may bring. While I know You are in heaven, I also know You are in my heart. Help me to realize how close You are to me every waking minute of this new day, a day You have made. Amen.

Now it's your turn. . . .

Lord, here's what I'm saying as I pray this line of the prayer: _____

_____

_____

_____ *Amen.*

The Prayer of Surrender: *"Your kingdom come, your will be done, on earth as it is in heaven"*

Our world is broken and dysfunctional. Bad things happen to good people. Sin is all around us. So it's hard to imagine "on earth as it is in heaven." God's kingdom is a place of perfect justice and truth, and at the end of time, all things will be restored. All injustices will be set right, all sins will be forgiven, and all illnesses will be healed.[6] But could this be a reality today? For young believers like thirty-three-year-old Briana, praying this verse is hard.

In 2004, a freak accident just two miles from her home in Wilber, Nebraska, changed her life forever. As she rumbled down a one-lane gravel road that cut through rolling farmland, a speeding pickup appeared in her path. Briana twisted her steering wheel, narrowly missing the oncoming truck but launching her own truck into a ditch.

"Here's the hardest part," explains Briana. "I never lost consciousness as the accident was happening. I remember every second—every detail of something I wish I could forget. And when my pickup stopped rolling, I heard the other truck drive away. At that point, I knew I was in the middle of nowhere. . .stranded."

Injured, alone, and left for dead on the side of the road is more trauma than most people can handle. Yet Briana was both physically and emotionally strong. In fact, she worked as an EMT (emergency medical technician) paramedic and was trained to keep her cool during stressful moments. It was the heartless act of two men fleeing the scene that really shook her up. And to add insult to injury, Briana's challenges went from bad to worse in the days that followed. Once she was stabilized, doctors explained that her back had been broken and her spinal cord injured. She needed multiple surgeries and months of rehab and faced the strong possibility of spending the rest of her days in a wheelchair.

"I was young and in the prime of my life," Briana says. "I had no clue that anything like that could happen to me. I had tested for the fire department the week before. It was crazy. The thought of never walking again was more than I could handle."

Briana soon spiraled deep into the fear-worry-anxiety cycle. At night, horrific images stole the rest she desperately needed. During the day, catastrophic thoughts gripped her mind: *What if my fiancé stops loving me? What if I can't pay all these medical bills? What if I have to depend on others to do everything for me? What if?*

Yet with the support of her family and her church, Briana is healing—physically, emotionally, and spiritually. And those profound words—"on earth as it is in heaven"—are more meaningful now than at any other time in her life.

She has discovered that even when all seems out of control, Jesus has never left us—and He never will! She prays confidently the prayer of surrender: "It's Your day, and I want Your will to be done. So whatever happens, hold my hand and let's face it together."

The simplicity of this prayer as we start our day brings freedom and a peace that passes understanding. And that's where God wants our heart. He wants us to be at peace and confident that whatever happens during the day can be handled. . .together.

The Bible tells us that in this world we will have trouble (John 16:33). But with Jesus at the center of our universe (instead of ourselves), we can be confident that He has overcome the world. With that assurance firmly implanted in our heart, we can face anything the world or our circumstances bring our way.

A Point to Ponder: Let's face it: life is fragile, messy, unpredictable, and sometimes tumultuous—just as Jesus said it would be. But if our focus is on God's will and *His* kingdom, then the prayer "I surrender all" is the perfect way to start each day. It's ultimately the secret of the surrendered life.

Living the Lord's Prayer

Lord, here's what I'm saying as I pray this line of the prayer: _____

_____

_____

_____

_____*Amen.*

What Is Needful: "Give us today our daily bread"

God takes care of us no matter what the situation may be. He is omniscient and knows what we need (Matthew 6:8, 32). He is omnipresent and is with us in every circumstance of life, "an ever-present help in trouble" (Psalm 46:1). He is omnipotent and "able to do immeasurably more than all we ask or imagine" (Ephesians 3:20). And according to Warren Wiersbe, God knows our needs better than we do, but He waits for us to ask. "True prayer is an act of faith, and God honors faith," Wiersbe writes. " 'If you believe,' said Jesus, 'you will receive whatever you ask for in prayer' (Matthew 21:22). Charles Spurgeon was correct when he said, 'Whether we like it or not, asking is the rule of the kingdom.' James agreed with him: 'You do not have because you do not ask God' (James 4:2)."[7]

Yet once in a while, scripture is profound in what it leaves out. In this line of the Lord's Prayer, Jesus doesn't ask us to pray the prayer of a full pantry and large bank account. Why? Worldwide, that's really a dumb prayer. It would have no basis in reality in half of the world's countries. So He keeps it simple: "Ask Me for today. Ask Me for sustenance today, for peace today, for *Me* today, for whatever. . .today, and that's a prayer I promise to answer."

That's the faith journey we all must live to become grateful followers who trust in the provision of our Father. But what of those praying this prayer who don't have bread, who don't have a roof, who don't have clean water to drink? This is the unfortunate dilemma as it relates to this passage: The sin of those who hoard their abundance affects the answer to the prayer of need. The truth is there *is* enough food to feed the world; there *is* enough money to pay for clean water; there *are* enough resources to care for and house the orphan. But the sin of the hoarders is that they are not open to being good stewards of all they have—which would mean sharing their abundance.

"We are God's stewards, not only of the human, animal, vegetable, and mineral blessings of His 'old creation,' " Wiersbe adds, "but also of the spiritual blessings of the 'new creation,' to which we belong as followers of Jesus Christ (2 Corinthians 5:17). One day we will have to give an account of our stewardship before the Lord (Romans 14:10–12), so we had better be faithful."[8]

Are you willing to be an answer to someone else's prayer for daily bread?

A Point to Ponder: Jesus Christ reminds us that He meets our needs: *"Do not worry about your life, what you will eat or drink; or about your body, what you will wear. Is not life more than food, and the body more than clothes? Look at the birds of the air; they do not sow or reap or store away in barns, and yet your heavenly Father feeds them. Are you not much more valuable than they? Can any one of you by worrying add a single hour to your life?" (Matthew 6:25–27).*

Living the Lord's Prayer:

Lord, here's what I'm saying as I pray this line of the prayer: _____

_____

_____

_____

_____*Amen.*

Accepting Our Nature: "And forgive us our debts"

Eighteen-year-old Porter of Colorado Springs just can't forgive himself for how he treated his parents. He stormed out of their lives in anger and then moved in with his girlfriend. Three months later, that relationship also fell apart. Even though he has confessed his sins to God—and has done his best to repair the damage he caused—the guilt is still there. He can't forget his stupid choices. He can't seem to forgive himself.

Welcome to the human race. Not only does the Bible say, "All have sinned and fall short of the glory of God" (Romans

3:23), but it also *doesn't* say, "All who come to faith don't sin and don't continue to need a Savior."

Our specific sins are, and our sin nature is, a minute-by-minute reminder that the whole human race has the same disease. To find success spiritually is to be comfortable with this fact: that while we don't want to sin so that grace may abound, we are still stuck in the muck of our nature—and that will never completely change no matter how much we wish it would. While we may have learned the secret of not sinning quite so much, what we often learn is how to hide it better than those outside the household of faith.

What separates those who have trusted Jesus as their Savior from those who haven't isn't an ability to sin less, but the knowledge that our sin has been forgiven and we can be free of its ongoing consequences: guilt and shame.

Allowing Jesus to transform our hearts and minds means having the ability to "forget what lies behind" and to "throw off the sin that so easily entangles us" (see Philippians 3:13; Hebrews 12:1). It means humbly asking God each day to clean out the pipeline between He and us and starting fresh. The Bible tells us the truth about yesterday's sins: "I [the LORD] will forgive their wickedness and will remember their sins no more" (Jeremiah 31:34).

It is said that "hurt people *hurt* people." Yet don't you think that broken individuals would begin treating others (and themselves) better if they knew they were forgiven? That's the power of knowing you're forgiven versus living with shame so deep it affects your ability to live strongly *today*.

We don't ever want to be content with keeping on in poor behaviors the Bible says are bad for our soul. A greater appreciation of morality (and a greater effort to uphold moral standards) enables God to use us more effectively in the world. A focus on morality helps us to quit thinking about how to please ourselves (which usually leads to sin) and start thinking about how to serve others. Sinning less allows us to focus on others, fulfilling the Great Commandment. Sadly, Christians have made morality a badge of honor as a way to separate us from those God has called us to love and serve.

Accepting our sin nature is of huge benefit in keeping us humble and connected to the Savior, but even more so in helping us shift our focus off ourselves and onto the lives of those outside the kingdom.

> *A Point to Ponder:* *All* are broken, but only a few admit it. The truth is, God doesn't expect us to have it all together; it's okay to be broken. The Lord is our Healer. He can accomplish in us what we cannot do on our own. He will clean out all the junk that weighs us down: our pride, our shame, our stubborn will—our tendency, as Paul wrote, to do "what I do not want to do." And the act of asking for forgiveness will help us learn the secrets of sinning less so that we can take our eyes off ourselves and love others with greater fervency.

Living the Lord's Prayer:

Lord, here's what I'm saying as I pray this line of the prayer: _____

_____

_____

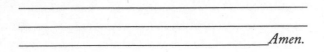

_____

_____

_____*Amen.*

Getting Untangled: "As we also have forgiven our debtors"

Unforgiveness keeps us in the past emotionally. It is a prison we put ourselves in, and only we hold the key to set us free. If receiving the supernatural and unmerited forgiveness of God is taking part of the divine nature of God, then forgiving those who have wronged us is giving away the divine nature of God. Remember: Jesus shares our pain. He puts Himself in our shoes and feels everything that we feel. He is the Father of "suffering with," and the God of all comfort! And when He comes beside us and offers the strength to take our next step, we learn to walk with fellow sufferers—to let their pain become your pain. We learn to forgive as He forgives.

> ***A Point to Ponder:*** We should strive to forgive as God forgives and to see others the way He sees them: lost but greatly loved by the One who longs for them to be redeemed through the blood of Jesus Christ. When we do that, we share in His divine nature and give away that same nature to those who need it most.

Living the Lord's Prayer

Lord, here's what I'm saying as I pray this line of the prayer: _____

_____

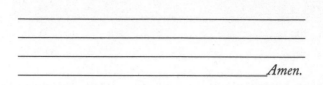

_____

_____

_____

_____*Amen.*

Free to Grow: *"And do not lead us into temptation"*

Not a single Christian hasn't struggled in one way or another with temptation and the enticement of sin. It's simply a part of life and something we'll always face regardless of how old we are. The good news is, God tells us—from the beginning of the Bible to the end—that He has overcome the trials and tribulations of this world. (Remember our conversation in chapter 5, "The Secret of Victorious Living"?) We are no longer slaves to them. As His children, we can be free!

But it can't happen on our own.

A relationship in close communication with Jesus is the only way to live—the only way to overcome temptation. The apostle Paul knew this all too well: "Not that I have already obtained all this, or have already arrived at my goal," he wrote, meaning he had never become complete and mature (Philippians 3:12). Instead, Paul had a realistic view of himself. He knew that because he was human, he had an innate tendency to sin. "Therefore, just as sin entered the world through one man, and death through sin, and in this way death came to all people, because all sinned—to be sure, sin was in the world before the law was given" (Romans 5:12–13).

Yes, the life-changing power of Christ was in his heart, but Paul knew he wouldn't reach perfection on this side of eternity. While Jesus' sacrifice on the cross delivered him from the ugly grip of sin and death, the finality of that deliverance would come only *after* this earthly life. He knew where he needed to be: on his knees, experiencing God's grace.

Paul knew that as we abide in Jesus, Christ lives through us. This relationship is dynamic, real, and personal. Jesus had an intimate relationship with the Father, and He intends for us to know that we can be one in and with Him. This is the great invitation to be a holy people, not in our efforts, abilities, or energies, but in a death to self, so that He might live in us moment by moment. Without Him in this moment, nothing but darkness remains.

> ***A Point to Ponder:*** We're not alone in our battle with temptation and sin, yet we have to understand and overcome the destructive forces at work in all our lives. That's the first step toward avoiding sin's disastrous consequences. The next is this: Get your eyes off yourself and consider how your sin affects others. When we succumb to temptation, the effects of our actions ripple in eternity. In considering the needs of others, we place the higher goal of caring for the souls of those we love above the fear and guilt of messing up morally.

Living the Lord's Prayer

Lord, here's what I'm saying as I pray this line of the prayer: _____

_____

_____

_____

_____

_____ _Amen._

Making It Personal: *"But deliver us from the evil one"*

Even though sin is not our master because we have the power of the Holy Spirit on our side, another force is still at work in our lives; it's a force that seeks to destroy our relationship with Christ, distort the truth, and block spiritual growth. I'm talking, of course, about Satan.

His very name means "accuser," and despite what some within the Church may think, the Scriptures do not portray him as a mere metaphor or symbol of evil. Satan is a created being who rebelled against God. He is very real, very dangerous, and is at work in the world today, enticing his victims toward evil.

The Bible refers to him as a deceiver (Revelation 12:9), an inciter (1 Chronicles 21:1), an accuser (Zechariah 3:1), a sinner (1 John 3:8), and a murderer and a liar (John 8:44). Scripture makes it clear that he is pure evil. Satan and his troops are viciously attacking the kingdom of God. His target: our souls.

"He can and will attempt to drag you down into such deep bondage that you will lose your joy in living," writes Charles Stanley in his book *When the Enemy Strikes*. "Some may call this bondage oppression, depression, or addiction. If the devil can pull you into bondage, you will have no peace, no zest for living, and perhaps even no will to continue living."[9]

A Point to Ponder: We are sensitive to heat, cold, pressure, and pain—and we go to great lengths to protect ourselves from their effects. But our ability to be spiritually sensitive to evil has been numbed because of (1) ambivalence, (2) failure to seek forgiveness from God, and (3) failure to recognize those behaviors that God says rob our soul of life. (Consider the current habit of rebellion against reading and applying the Bible). Developing sensitivity to evil and to the evil one—not just to sin and bad choices— acknowledges the battle we are truly engaged in. If we had our guard up a bit more and were not ignorant of the devil's schemes, our discernment would then be heightened enough to recognize the way of escape God always provides for us to win over temptation (see 1 Corinthians 10:13; 2 Corinthians 2:11). Usually just a word— "begone."

Living the Lord's Prayer

Lord, here's what I'm saying as I pray this line of the prayer: _____

_____

_____

_____

_____ *Amen.*

9

PRAYING THE PSALMS

"LORD, help!" they cried in their trouble, and he saved them from
their distress. He calmed the storm to a whisper and stilled the waves.
What a blessing was that stillness as he brought them safely into harbor!

PSALM 107:28–30 NLT

It's known as the songbook of scripture—there are 150 in all—
and it's right in the heart of the Bible. Although we no longer
have the original music to accompany each piece, they've been
sung for thousands of years a cappella and with instruments. In
addition to the songs and poems found here, the book of Psalms
is scripture's go-to place for prayer. Whether we're in trouble and
need the Lord to intervene or we want to offer up praise for the
good things God has done, so many of our needs are expressed
here.

According to scholars, there are twelve different types of
psalms. Here's how they are officially identified: (1) prayers of the
individual; (2) praise from the individual for God's saving help;
(3) prayers of the community; (4) praise from the community
for God's saving help; (5) confessions of confidence in the Lord;
(6) hymns in praise of God's majesty and virtues; (7) hymns
celebrating God's universal reign; (8) songs of Zion, the city of
God; (9) royal psalms—by, for, or concerning the king, the Lord's
anointed; (10) pilgrimage songs; (11) liturgical songs; and (12)
didactic—instructional—songs.[1]

Among the collections of prayers are different categories,
including prayers of adoration and praise, confessions, laments,

appeals for protection, as well as joyful expressions of supplication and thanksgiving.

We've included some popular psalms within this chapter. As you explore these timeless passages, make them part of your prayer time with God.

In Awe of the Almighty: Adoration and Praise

As the Psalms appropriately share, our God is an awesome God. He is worthy of our adoration, praise, reverence, and utmost respect. He is pleased when we express our appreciation, and James 4:8 tells us, "Come near to God and he will come near to you." This collection of prayers can help us praise God for His mercy and everlasting love.

Psalm 8

LORD, our Lord, how majestic is your name in all the earth!

You have set your glory in the heavens. Through the praise of children and infants you have established a stronghold against your enemies, to silence the foe and the avenger. When I consider your heavens, the work of your fingers, the moon and the stars, which you have set in place, what is mankind that you are mindful of them, human beings that you care for them?

You have made them a little lower than the angels and crowned them with glory and honor. You made them rulers over the works of your hands; you put everything under their feet: all flocks and herds, and the animals of the wild, the birds in the sky, and the fish in the sea, all that swim the paths of the seas.

LORD, our Lord, how majestic is your name in all the earth!

Psalm 30

I will exalt you, LORD, for you lifted me out of the depths and did not let my enemies gloat over me. LORD my God, I called to you for help, and you healed me. You, LORD, brought me up from the realm of the dead; you spared me from going down to the pit.

Sing the praises of the LORD, you his faithful people; praise his holy name. For his anger lasts only a moment, but his favor lasts a lifetime; weeping may stay for the night, but rejoicing comes in the morning.

When I felt secure, I said, "I will never be shaken." LORD, when you favored me, you made my royal mountain stand firm; but when you hid your face, I was dismayed.

To you, LORD, I called; to the Lord I cried for mercy: "What is gained if I am silenced, if I go down to the pit? Will the dust praise you? Will it proclaim your faithfulness? Hear, LORD, and be merciful to me; LORD, be my help."

You turned my wailing into dancing; you removed my sackcloth and clothed me with joy, that my heart may sing your praises and not be silent. LORD my God, I will praise you forever.

Psalm 138 MSG

Thank you! Everything in me says "Thank you!" Angels listen as I sing my thanks. I kneel in worship facing your holy temple and say it again: "Thank you!" Thank you for your love, thank you for your faithfulness; most holy is your name, most holy is your Word. The moment I called out, you stepped in; you made my life large with strength.

When they hear what you have to say, GOD, all earth's kings will say "Thank you." They'll sing of what you've done: "How great the glory of GOD!" And here's why: GOD, high above, sees far below; no matter the distance, he knows everything about us.

When I walk into the thick of trouble, keep me alive in the angry turmoil. With one hand strike my foes, with your other hand save me. Finish what you started in me, GOD. Your love is eternal—don't quit on me now.

Psalm 139 NASB

O LORD, You have searched me and known me. You know when I sit down and when I rise up; You understand my thought from afar. You scrutinize my path and my lying down, and are intimately acquainted with all my ways. Even before there is a word on my tongue, behold, O LORD, You know it all. You have enclosed me behind and before, and laid Your hand upon me. Such knowledge is too wonderful for me; it is too high, I cannot attain to it.

Where can I go from Your Spirit? Or where can I flee from Your presence? If I ascend to heaven, You are there; if I make my bed in Sheol, behold, You are there. If I take the wings of the dawn, if I dwell in the remotest part of the sea, even there Your hand will lead me, and Your right hand will lay hold of me. If I say, "Surely the darkness will overwhelm me, and the light around me will be night," even the darkness is not dark to You, and the night is as bright as the day. Darkness and light are alike to You.

For You formed my inward parts; You wove me in my mother's womb. I will give thanks to You, for I am fearfully and wonderfully made; wonderful are Your works, and my soul knows it very well. My frame was not hidden from You, when I was made in secret, and skillfully wrought in the depths of the earth; Your eyes have seen my unformed substance; and in Your book were all written the days that were ordained for me, when as yet there was not one of them.

How precious also are Your thoughts to me, O God! How vast is the sum of them! If I should count them, they would outnumber the sand. When I awake, I am still with You.

O that You would slay the wicked, O God; depart from me, therefore, men of bloodshed. For they speak against You wickedly, and Your enemies take Your name in vain. Do I not hate those who hate You, O LORD? And do I not loathe those who rise up against You? I hate them with the utmost hatred; they have become my enemies.

Search me, O God, and know my heart; try me and know my anxious thoughts; and see if there be any hurtful way in me, and lead me in the everlasting way.

Coming Clean with God: Prayers of Confession

The Bible offers prayers of confession that cover two different topics: confession of sin and confession of faith. We've selected two psalms to guide you as you acknowledge your sin before God. We encourage you to flip back to chapter 4, "Confession: Regaining Intimacy with God," for a deeper look at this type of prayer. As you pray these psalms, keep in mind what we explained earlier: confession involves four steps: (1) admitting your sin, (2) grieving your actions and telling God you're sorry, (3) asking Him to forgive you and cleanse you, and (4) telling God you want to repent and follow Him.

Psalm 32 ESV

Blessed is the one whose transgression is forgiven, whose sin is covered. Blessed is the man against whom the LORD counts no iniquity, and in whose spirit there is no deceit.

For when I kept silent, my bones wasted away through my groaning all day long. For day and night your hand was heavy upon me; my strength was dried up as by the heat of summer. I acknowledged my sin to you, and I did not cover my iniquity; I said, "I will confess my transgressions to the LORD," and you forgave the iniquity of my sin.

Therefore let everyone who is godly offer prayer to you at a time when you may be found; surely in the rush of great waters, they shall not reach him. You are a hiding place for me; you preserve me from trouble; you surround me with shouts of deliverance.

I will instruct you and teach you in the way you

should go; I will counsel you with my eye upon you. Be not like a horse or a mule, without understanding, which must be curbed with bit and bridle, or it will not stay near you.

Many are the sorrows of the wicked, but steadfast love surrounds the one who trusts in the LORD. Be glad in the LORD, and rejoice, O righteous, and shout for joy, all you upright in heart!

Psalm 51:1–12

Have mercy on me, O God, according to your unfailing love; according to your great compassion blot out my transgressions. Wash away all my iniquity and cleanse me from my sin.

For I know my transgressions, and my sin is always before me. Against you, you only, have I sinned and done what is evil in your sight; so you are right in your verdict and justified when you judge. Surely I was sinful at birth, sinful from the time my mother conceived me. Yet you desired faithfulness even in the womb; you taught me wisdom in that secret place.

Cleanse me with hyssop, and I will be clean; wash me, and I will be whiter than snow. Let me hear joy and gladness; let the bones you have crushed rejoice. Hide your face from my sins and blot out all my iniquity.

Create in me a pure heart, O God, and renew a steadfast spirit within me. Do not cast me from your presence or take your Holy Spirit from me. Restore to me the joy of your salvation and grant me a willing spirit, to sustain me.

A Time to Weep: Biblical Laments

Here's how *Merriam-Webster* defines the word *lament*: "to mourn aloud: wail; to express sorrow, mourning; to regret strongly." You'll discover passages in the Psalms in which the brokenhearted pour out their pain in lament to God. They capture the agony so many of us have felt at least once in our lives. As you read and pray through them, keep in mind that a lament is a form of worship and faith.

Psalm 13

How long, LORD? Will you forget me forever? How long will you hide your face from me? How long must I wrestle with my thoughts and day after day have sorrow in my heart? How long will my enemy triumph over me? Look on me and answer, LORD my God. Give light to my eyes, or I will sleep in death, and my enemy will say, "I have overcome him," and my foes will rejoice when I fall.

But I trust in your unfailing love; my heart rejoices in your salvation. I will sing the LORD's praise, for he has been good to me.

Psalm 30 NLT

I will exalt you, LORD, for you rescued me. You refused to let my enemies triumph over me. O LORD my God, I cried to you for help, and you restored my health. You brought me up from the grave, O LORD. You kept me from falling into the pit of death.

Sing to the LORD, all you godly ones! Praise his holy name. For his anger lasts only a moment, but his favor lasts a lifetime! Weeping may last through the night, but joy comes with the morning.

When I was prosperous, I said, "Nothing can stop me now!" Your favor, O LORD, made me as secure as a mountain. Then you turned away from me, and I was shattered.

I cried out to you, O LORD. I begged the Lord for mercy, saying, "What will you gain if I die, if I sink into the grave? Can my dust praise you? Can it tell of your faithfulness? Hear me, LORD, and have mercy on me. Help me, O LORD."

You have turned my mourning into joyful dancing. You have taken away my clothes of mourning and clothed me with joy, that I might sing praises to you and not be silent. O LORD my God, I will give you thanks forever!

When Danger Lurks: Prayers of Protection

More than seventeen times in the Gospels, the Greek word for "salvation" is linked to the meaning of "physical rescue from harm or danger." We've observed this connection in the book of Psalms as well. As you pray these passages, keep in mind that God is our Creator, Father, Savior, Provider, and Protector.

Psalm 25

In you, LORD my God, I put my trust.

I trust in you; do not let me be put to shame, nor let my enemies triumph over me. No one who hopes in you will ever be put to shame, but shame will come on those who are treacherous without cause.

Show me your ways, LORD, teach me your paths.

Guide me in your truth and teach me, for you are God my Savior, and my hope is in you all day long. Remember, LORD, your great mercy and love, for they are from of old. Do not remember the sins of my youth and my rebellious ways; according to your love remember me, for you, LORD, are good.

Good and upright is the LORD; therefore he instructs sinners in his ways. He guides the humble in what is right and teaches them his way. All the ways of the LORD are loving and faithful toward those who keep the demands of his covenant. For the sake of your name, LORD, forgive my iniquity, though it is great.

Who, then, are those who fear the LORD? He will instruct them in the ways they should choose. They will spend their days in prosperity, and their descendants will inherit the land. The LORD confides in those who fear him; he makes his covenant known to them. My eyes are ever on the LORD, for only he will release my feet from the snare.

Turn to me and be gracious to me, for I am lonely and afflicted. Relieve the troubles of my heart and free me from my anguish. Look on my affliction and my distress and take away all my sins. See how numerous are my enemies and how fiercely they hate me!

Guard my life and rescue me; do not let me be put to shame, for I take refuge in you. May integrity and uprightness protect me, because my hope, LORD, is in you.

Deliver Israel, O God, from all their troubles!

Psalm 140 MSG

GOD, get me out of here, away from this evil; protect me from these vicious people. All they do is think up new ways to be bad; they spend their days plotting war games. They practice the sharp rhetoric of hate and hurt, speak venomous words that maim and kill. GOD, keep me out of the clutch of these wicked ones, protect me from these vicious people; stuffed with self-importance, they plot ways to trip me up, determined to bring me down. These crooks invent traps to catch me and do their best to incriminate me.

I prayed, "GOD, you're my God! Listen, GOD! Mercy! GOD, my Lord, Strong Savior, protect me when the fighting breaks out! Don't let the wicked have their way, GOD, don't give them an inch!"

These troublemakers all around me—let them drown in their own verbal poison. Let God pile hellfire on them, let him bury them alive in crevasses! These loudmouths—don't let them be taken seriously, these savages—let the Devil hunt them down!

I know that you, GOD, are on the side of victims, that you care for the rights of the poor. And I know that the righteous personally thank you, that good people are secure in your presence.

Presenting Needs: Prayers of Supplication

The word *supplication* is often associated with the humble act of asking for or even begging for something. In the Old Testament, the Hebrew word communicates the idea of "humbling oneself"—usually in prayer. And that's the meaning in these passages. As we pray in supplication, we are asking God to make our minds "supple" so He can make us like Christ and mold us into the person He wants us to be.

Psalm 6

Lord, do not rebuke me in your anger or discipline me in your wrath. Have mercy on me, Lord, for I am faint; heal me, Lord, for my bones are in agony. My soul is in deep anguish. How long, Lord, how long? Turn, Lord, and deliver me; save me because of your unfailing love. Among the dead no one proclaims your name. Who praises you from the grave?

I am worn out from my groaning.

All night long I flood my bed with weeping and drench my couch with tears. My eyes grow weak with sorrow; they fail because of all my foes.

Away from me, all you who do evil, for the Lord has heard my weeping. The Lord has heard my cry for mercy; the Lord accepts my prayer. All my enemies will be overwhelmed with shame and anguish; they will turn back and suddenly be put to shame.

Psalm 86 NLT

Bend down, O Lord, and hear my prayer; answer me, for I need your help. Protect me, for I am devoted to you. Save me, for I serve you and trust you. You are my God. Be merciful to me, O Lord, for I am calling on you constantly. Give me happiness, O Lord, for I give myself to you. O Lord, you are so good, so ready to forgive, so full of unfailing love for all who ask for your help. Listen closely to my prayer, O LORD; hear my urgent cry. I will call to you whenever I'm in trouble, and you will answer me.

No pagan god is like you, O Lord. None can do what you do! All the nations you made will come and bow before you, Lord; they will praise your holy name. For you are great and perform wonderful deeds. You alone are God.

Teach me your ways, O LORD, that I may live according to your truth! Grant me purity of heart, so that I may honor you. With all my heart I will praise you, O Lord my God. I will give glory to your name forever, for your love for me is very great. You have rescued me from the depths of death.

O God, insolent people rise up against me; a violent gang is trying to kill me. You mean nothing to them. But you, O Lord, are a God of compassion and mercy, slow to get angry and filled with unfailing love and faithfulness. Look down and have mercy on me. Give your strength to your servant; save me, the son of your servant. Send me a sign of your favor. Then those who hate me will be put to shame, for you, O LORD, help and comfort me.

Expressing a Joyful Heart: Prayers of Thanksgiving

We find prayers of thanksgiving all throughout the Bible. As we express them, we remember all that God has done for us and thank Him with a sincere heart.

Psalm 34 MSG

I bless GOD every chance I get; my lungs expand

with his praise. I live and breathe GOD; if things aren't going well, hear this and be happy: Join me in spreading the news; together let's get the word out. GOD met me more than halfway, he freed me from my anxious fears. Look at him; give him your warmest smile. Never hide your feelings from him. When I was desperate, I called out, and GOD got me out of a tight spot. GOD's angel sets up a circle of protection around us while we pray. Open your mouth and taste, open your eyes and see—how good GOD is. Blessed are you who run to him. Worship GOD if you want the best; worship opens doors to all his goodness. Young lions on the prowl get hungry, but GOD-seekers are full of God. Come, children, listen closely; I'll give you a lesson in GOD worship. Who out there has a lust for life? Can't wait each day to come upon beauty? Guard your tongue from profanity, and no more lying through your teeth. Turn your back on sin; do something good. Embrace peace—don't let it get away! GOD keeps an eye on his friends, his ears pick up every moan and groan. GOD won't put up with rebels; he'll cull them from the pack. Is anyone crying for help? GOD is listening, ready to rescue you. If your heart is broken, you'll find GOD right there; if you're kicked in the gut, he'll help you catch your breath. Disciples so often get into trouble; still, GOD is there every time. He's your bodyguard, shielding every bone; not even a finger gets broken. The wicked commit slow suicide; they waste their lives hating the good. GOD pays for each slave's freedom; no one who runs to him loses out.

Psalm 136

Give thanks to the Lord, for he is good.
His love endures forever.
Give thanks to the God of gods.
His love endures forever.
Give thanks to the Lord of lords:
His love endures forever.
to him who alone does great wonders,
His love endures forever.
who by his understanding made the heavens,
His love endures forever.
who spread out the earth upon the waters,
His love endures forever.
who made the great lights—
His love endures forever.
the sun to govern the day,
His love endures forever.
the moon and stars to govern the night;
His love endures forever. . . .
He remembered us in our low estate
His love endures forever.
and freed us from our enemies.
His love endures forever.
He gives food to every creature.
His love endures forever.
Give thanks to the God of heaven.
His love endures forever.

Madame Guyon on Praying the Scripture

"Praying the Scripture" is a unique way of dealing with Scripture; it involves both reading and prayer. Turn to the Scripture; choose some passage that is simple and fairly practical. Next, come to the Lord. Come quietly and humbly. There, before him, read a small portion of the passage of Scripture you have opened to.

Be careful as you read. Take in fully, gently, and carefully what you are reading. Taste it and digest it as you read. In the past it may have been your habit, while reading, to move very quickly from one verse of Scripture to another until you have read the whole passage. Perhaps you were seeking to find the main point of the passage.

But in coming to the Lord by means of "praying the Scripture," you do not read quickly; you read very slowly. You do not move from one passage to another, not until you have *sensed* the very heart of what you have read. You may then want to take that portion of Scripture that has touched you and turn it into prayer.

After you have sensed something of the passage, and after you know that the essence of that portion has been extracted and all the deeper sense of it is gone, then, very slowly, gently, and in a calm manner begin to read the next portion of that passage. You will be surprised to find that when your time with the Lord has ended, you will have read very little, probably no more than half a page.[2]

10

HISTORY'S FAMOUS PRAYERS

A Prayer for All Believers by Jesus Christ

My prayer is not for them alone. I pray also for those
who will believe in me through their message, that all
of them may be one, Father, just as you are in me and
I am in you. May they also be in us so that the world
may believe that you have sent me. I have given them
the glory that you gave me, that they may be one as we
are one—I in them and you in me—so that they may
be brought to complete unity. Then the world will know
that you sent me and have loved them even as you have
loved me. (John 17:20–23)

The Lord's Prayer by John Bunyan

Our Father which in heaven art,
Thy name be always hallowed;
Thy kingdom come, thy will be done;
Thy heavenly path be followed:
By us on earth, as 'tis with thee,
We humbly pray;
And let our bread us given be
From day to day.
Forgive our debts, as we forgive
Those that to us indebted are;
Into temptation lead us not;
But save us from the wicked snare.
The kingdom's thine, the power too,

We thee adore;
The glory shall be thine
For evermore.[1]

A Prayer of Confession by John Calvin

O Lord God, eternal and almighty Father, we acknowledge and sincerely confess before your holy majesty that we are miserable sinners, conceived and born in iniquity and sin, prone to evil, and incapable of any good work, and that in our depravity we make no end of breaking your holy commandments. We thus call down destruction on ourselves from your just judgments. Nevertheless, O Lord, we lament that we have offended you, and we condemn ourselves and our faults with true repentance, asking you to help us from wretchedness by your grace.

Deign, then, O most gracious and most merciful God and Father, to bestow your mercy on us in the name of Jesus Christ your Son our Lord. Effacing our faults, and all our sinfulness, daily increase on us the gifts of your Holy Spirit, that we from our inner hearts, acknowledging our sin, may be more and more displeasing to ourselves, and become truly repentant, and that your Holy Spirit may produce in us the fruits of righteousness and holiness, through Jesus Christ, our Savior.[2]

A Prayer for Deeper Faith by Malcolm Muggeridge

O God, stay with me; let no word cross my lips that is not your word, no thoughts enter my mind that are not your thoughts, no deed ever be done or entertained by me that is not your deed.[3]

A Salvation Prayer by Jonah

Then Jonah prayed to his God from the belly of the fish. He prayed: "In trouble, deep trouble, I prayed to GOD. He answered me. From the belly of the grave I cried, 'Help!' You heard my cry. You threw me into ocean's depths, into a watery grave, with ocean waves, ocean breakers crashing over me. I said, 'I've been thrown away, thrown out, out of your sight. I'll never again lay eyes on your Holy Temple.' Ocean gripped me by the throat. The ancient Abyss grabbed me and held tight. My head was all tangled in seaweed at the bottom of the sea where the mountains take root. I was as far down as a body can go, and the gates were slamming shut behind me forever—yet you pulled me up from that grave alive, O GOD, my God! When my life was slipping away, I remembered GOD, and my prayer got through to you, made it all the way to your Holy Temple. Those who worship hollow gods, god-frauds, walk away from their only true love. But I'm worshiping you, GOD, calling out in thanksgiving! And I'll do what I promised I'd do! Salvation belongs to GOD!" (Jonah 2:1–9 MSG)

The "Breastplate Prayer" Inspired by St. Patrick

Christ with me,
Christ before me,
Christ behind me,
Christ in me,
Christ beneath me,
Christ above me,
Christ on my right,
Christ on my left,
Christ when I lie down,
Christ when I sit down,
Christ when I arise,
Christ in the heart of every man who thinks of me,
Christ in the mouth of everyone who speaks of me,
Christ in every eye that sees me,
Christ in every ear that hears me.
I arise today
Through a mighty strength, the invocation of the Trinity,
Through belief in the Threeness,
Through confession of the Oneness
of the Creator of creation.[4]

A Morning Prayer by Ogden Nash

Now another day is breaking;
sleep was sweet, and so is waking.
Dear Lord, I promised you last night
never again to sulk or fight.
Such vows are easier to keep
when a child is sound asleep.
Today, O Lord, for your dear sake,
I'll try to keep them when awake.[5]

An Evening Prayer by Dietrich Bonhoeffer

O Lord my God, I thank you that you have brought this day to a close; I thank you that you have given me peace in body and soul. Your hand has been over me and has protected and preserved me. Forgive my puny faith, the ill that I this day have done, and help me to forgive all who have wronged me. Grant me a quiet night's sleep beneath your tender care. And defend me from all the temptations of darkness. Into your hands I commend my loved ones and all who dwell in this house; I commend my body and soul. O God, your holy name be praised. Amen.[6]

A Prayer to Be Christ's Witness by Mother Teresa

Dear Jesus, help us to spread your fragrance everywhere we go. Flood our souls with your spirit and life. Penetrate and possess our whole being so utterly that our lives may only be a radiance of yours. Shine through us and be so in us that every soul we come in contact with may feel your presence in our soul.

Let them look up and see no longer us, but only Jesus. Stay with us and then we shall begin to shine as you shine, so to shine as to be light to others. The light, O Jesus, will be all from you. None of it will be ours. It will be you shining on others through us.

Let us thus praise you in the way you love best by shining on those around us. Let us preach you without preaching, not by words, but by our example; by the catching force—the sympathetic influence of what we do, the evident fullness of the love our hearts bear to you. Amen.[7]

A Prayer to Draw Closer to God by Thomas à Kempis

In confidence of your goodness and great mercy, O Lord, I draw near to you, as a sick person to the Healer, as one hungry and thirsty to the Fountain of life, a creature to the Creator, a desolate soul to my own tender Comforter. Behold, in you is everything that I can or ought to desire. You are my salvation and my redemption, my Helper and my strength.[8]

A Prayer for Healing from *Common Prayer: A Liturgy for Ordinary Radicals*

In the name of the Father, and of the Son, and of the Holy Spirit, we enjoin your divine mercies. Lord, why do we suffer? Why do we hurt? Shall our only answer be the whirlwind of unknowing which engulfed Job? Why do the wicked flourish, while the righteous waste away? I am left speechless, left with the words, "I will trust in you, my God."

God, we ask for the sending of your healing Spirit, who came to us through Jesus, as he breathed upon his disciples. This Spirit gathered your people, to be warmed by the fire of divine presence. By this warmth, may *(name of person here)* be healed and taken into your care.

Like the blind man whom Jesus healed, may *(name of person here)* become a sign of your glory, calling you the Anointed One, the one who also anoints us and points us to the love of God. Grant us your healing peace. Amen.[9]

A Covenant Prayer by John Wesley

I am no longer my own, but thine. Put me to what thou wilt, rank me with whom thou wilt. Put me to doing, put me to suffering. Let me be employed for thee or laid aside for thee, exalted for thee or brought low for thee. Let me be full, let me be empty. Let me have all things, let me have nothing. I freely and heartily yield all things to thy pleasure and disposal. And now, O glorious and blessed God, Father, Son and Holy Spirit, thou art mine, and I am thine. So be it. And the covenant which I have made on earth, let it be ratified in heaven. Amen.[10]

A Prayer for Guidance by George Washington

O eternal and everlasting God, I presume to present myself this morning before thy Divine majesty, beseeching thee to accept of my humble and hearty thanks, that it hath pleased thy great goodness to keep and preserve me the night past from all the dangers poor mortals are subject to, and has given me sweet and pleasant sleep, whereby I find my body refreshed and comforted for performing the duties of this day, in which I beseech thee to defend me from all perils of body and soul.

Increase my faith in the sweet promises of the gospel; give me repentance from dead works; pardon my wanderings, and direct my thoughts unto thyself, the God of my salvation; teach me how to live in thy fear, labor in thy service, and ever to run in the ways of thy commandments; make me always watchful over my heart, that neither the terrors of conscience, the loathing of holy duties, the love of sin, nor an unwillingness to depart this life, may cast me into a spiritual slumber, but daily frame me more and more into the likeness of thy son Jesus Christ, that living in thy fear, and dying in thy favor, I may in thy appointed time attain the resurrection of the just unto eternal life. Bless my family, friends, and kindred.[11]

A Prayer for Deliverance by King David

LORD, how they have increased who trouble me! Many are they who rise up against me. Many are they who say of me, "There is no help for him in God."

But You, O LORD, are a shield for me, my glory and the One who lifts up my head. I cried to the LORD with my voice, and He heard me from His holy hill.

I lay down and slept; I awoke, for the LORD sustained me. I will not be afraid of ten thousands of people who have set themselves against me all around.

Arise, O LORD; save me, O my God! For You have struck all my enemies on the cheekbone; You have broken the teeth of the ungodly. Salvation belongs to the LORD. Your blessing is upon Your people. (Psalm 3 NKJV)

A Prayer for Families from *The Book of Common Prayer*

Almighty God, our heavenly Father, who settest the solitary in families: We commend to thy continual care the homes in which thy people dwell. Put far from them, we beseech thee, every root of bitterness, the desire of vainglory, and the pride of life. Fill them with faith, virtue, knowledge, temperance, patience, godliness. Knit together in constant affection those who, in holy wedlock, have been made one flesh. Turn the hearts of the parents to the children, and the hearts of the children to the parents; and so enkindle fervent charity among us all, that we may evermore be kindly affectioned one to another; through Jesus Christ our Lord. Amen.[12]

A Prayer for His Son by General Douglas MacArthur

Build me a son, O Lord, who will be strong enough to know when he is weak, and brave enough to face himself when he is afraid; one who will be proud and unbending in honest defeat, and humble and gentle in victory.

Build me a son whose wishbone will not be where his backbone should be; a son who will know Thee and that to know himself is the foundation stone of knowledge.

Lead him, I pray, not in the path of ease and comfort, but under the stress and spur of difficulties and challenge. Here let him learn to stand up in the storm; here let him learn compassion for those who fail.

Build me a son whose heart will be clean, whose goal will be high; a son who will master himself before he seeks to master other men; one who will learn to laugh, yet never forget how to weep; one who will reach into the future, yet never forget the past.

And after all these things are his, add, I pray, enough of a sense of humor so that he may always be serious, yet never take himself too seriously. Give him humility, so that he may always remember the simplicity of greatness, the open mind of true wisdom, the meekness of true strength. Then I, his father, will dare to whisper, "I have not lived in vain." Amen.[13]

A Prayer for a Fresh Start by Janet Lees

God of good ideas, who began the world with light and word, who began again with flood and rainbow; we acknowledge our frustration with your church: its committees and structures, its methods and systems. These things have made us angry and sapped our energy.

God of new beginnings who began a new way of living with resurrection, who began a new community with tongues of fire; begin again here that structures may bend like dancing saplings; that past, present, and future may be woven into a fresh path of commitment.

May our ideas for your world and this community resonate in your presence, so that tested, tried, and challenged they may blossom in us as do dry places when longed-for rain falls.[14]

Part Four

STORIES OF PRAYER

11

HOW TO PRAY. . .
WHEN ALL SEEMS LOST

"Then you will call on me and come and pray to me,
and I will listen to you."

JEREMIAH 29:12

"If anyone could possibly be too far gone for God—I'd be that person.
I was enslaved by a secret struggle that destroyed my life. . ."

Gone. Everyone he loved and everything he worked so hard to achieve in life had been ripped from him. The loss was almost too much to bear, yet Keith knew there was no one to blame but himself.

The forty-two-year-old Pennsylvania man curled up on a futon in his sister's basement (his temporary home) and read a passage of scripture that popped up on his cell phone. It was 1 Peter 1:14–15 (NLT): "So you must live as God's obedient children. Don't slip back into your old ways of living to satisfy your own desires. You didn't know any better then. But now you must be holy in everything you do, just as God who chose you is holy."

The words stung. But that's usually what happens as medicine penetrates a wound. Keith took a deep breath and squeezed his eyes shut. Everything was crystal clear now. It was obvious how he had gotten to this miserable point, and he regretted every selfish step.

"It all started when I chose to 'satisfy my own desires,' not the will of God," he remembers. "I had allowed myself to slip back into my old ways—just as scripture warns us not to do. I let sinful choices take over."

Eventually, those choices stole his family, his ministry, his money, and his reputation.

"It's one thing to make crazy decisions when we're young and naïve and inclined to learn the hard way," he says. "It's entirely different when we're middle-aged, supposedly 'seasoned in the faith,' and in my case, a *pastor*."

A secret struggle began to enslave him. And even though Keith put up a desperate fight to break free, his world caved in on top of him. "I brought shame on my kids and broke my wife's heart," he says. "The fact is, I had lied to everyone—over and over for so many years. That's hard to live with."

The Bible app on his phone chimed again, so he tapped the screen. More scripture: " 'Lord, help!' they cried in their trouble, and he saved them from their distress. He sent out his word and healed them, snatching them from the door of death" (Psalm 107:19–20 NLT).

This time, the words were soothing.

"Too often, our shame inside tries to convince us that we are worthless—too far gone for God," Keith admits. "But God's Word tells us something different. Verse after verse reveals how Christ feels about us. He forgives, heals, and restores. He snatches us from death's door. He loves us too much to ever let us go."

Keith's life will never be the same. Emotional wounds and vivid memories continually remind him of all he has lost. Old temptations kick in whenever he is weak. Yet after years of feeling trapped by sin, Keith has found freedom. What finally made the difference for him? The Bible. Restored prayer. The loving embrace of Christ-followers who simply won't give up on him.

"God's Word has been like an IV drip of truth in my life," he says. "The questions and scriptures I've been exploring lately nail my weaknesses. Every time I hear that familiar 'ping,' I stop what I'm doing and read the verse. Even if I'm driving, I pull over and tap my phone.

"Verse after verse is nudging me closer to Jesus, teaching me that He can redeem any sin," Keith adds. "The Lord is restoring my broken life, and He's using God's Word, lots of prayer, and lots and lots of tears to do it."

A Long Time Ago—in Another Life

Keith grew up in rural Pennsylvania in a non-Christian home. He went to church with his grandmother on the weekends and was exposed to the Gospel. He committed his life to Jesus when he was nine. And then the unexpected: his father died when he was twelve.

"It rocked my world when my dad past away," he says. "I was unprepared for that. My family was pretty messed up. As a kid, I thought about spiritual issues. . .and I knew my dad wasn't saved. That broke my heart."

It also made him think. About life after death. About eternity.

Is there a chance that my dad asked Jesus into his heart—maybe on his deathbed? Keith wondered. *Is there a chance I'll see him in heaven?*

Keith was tired of *chances*. It was time for action.

By high school, he sensed God calling him into full-time ministry. He had committed his life to being Christ's witness.

He couldn't bear the thought of his dad—or anyone—missing eternity with Jesus. "My giftedness is in music, so in my little one-horse town, I did everything I possibly could to grow my musical gifts. After graduation, I enrolled in a Christian college on the other side of the continent—in Southern California. That was a big step for me—moving from Pennsylvania to Los Angeles."

Moving from a small town to a big city was a culture shock. But Keith adjusted, and the years flew by. He graduated in 1995, with a degree in church music and was quickly recruited by a megachurch in Kansas City.

In 1998 he married Carly, and four years later their daughter Kimberly was born. Soon afterward, another large church knocked on his door. This one was in Santa Monica, California— back in the state he had grown to love.

"This was my third church. It was a big place, and I envisioned myself being there for life. It was a place where I thought my family could settle in. And by 2004, my family grew again: my son Carl was born."

But in 2007, everything came to a screeching halt.

"The Lord began to squeeze my heart," Keith says. "He crushed me into repentance."

The young worship pastor went to the elders at his church and confessed that he was struggling with homosexuality— something he'd engaged in secretly since his teen years.

His church had never dealt with a pastor who struggled with this issue, and the elders were at a loss over what to do.

"So they decided to rebuke me in the presence of all so that others would be fearful of sinning," Keith explains. "So on a Thursday morning, I kissed my wife good-bye and left the house, and by 3:00 p.m. I was unemployed. My ministry was over. I dropped a bomb on everyone.

"That Sunday, I confessed my struggles during two services," he adds. "It was a church of about one thousand people, so everyone responded in different ways. Some were angry. Others were mad at the elders, believing they handled this horribly. But a lot of people were furious with me. I had broken their trust. I led a double life and had lied to them."

Keith's wife was among those who were devastated, and their marriage ended a year later. It was twelve brutal months filled with counseling, long talks, begging, crying, and sleepless nights. "It happened in 2008, just three days shy of our ten-year anniversary," Keith says. "Carly took the kids and moved out."

Later she filed for divorce. So for the next four years, Keith lived with friends and did odd jobs just to survive. "My life had become a living horror."

There and Back Again

In 2012 Keith went to his doctor with serious flu-like symptoms. He was afraid of the prognosis. In his gut, he knew what was going on in his body. He knew that things had just gone from bad to worse.

"I was HIV positive," he admits. "Yet another horrible experience that once again rocked my world."

But during his darkest moment, Keith's cell phone chimed, and an unexpected voice from his past answered his greeting. The voice was inviting him to come home.

"Keith, it's Nikki—your sister."

At first, he was speechless. The two hadn't talked in years.

"I want you to come home—come back to Pennsylvania.

My life is different. . .better. And it's because of you. You helped me—eternally. And now it's my turn to help you."

Today, Keith sleeps on a futon in his sister's basement—his temporary home.

"Spiritually, I've gone from years and years of gutting through my struggles, trying to be better," he says, "but failing every single time. It's a cycle of constantly needing Christ's forgiveness. Knowing scripturally that I'm forgiven through Jesus Christ—I can trust in God's forgiveness through Jesus—but not really feeling it, not really experiencing it. It looks great on paper. And I can defend it on paper. But as far as believing it and living it out. . .at times, I just wasn't experiencing it."

He says that one of the freedoms that came from his confession of sin is that he has finally been able to settle down with people who know his sin—and who are just as horrified by it as he is—and yet who are still willing to love and accept him. "From the world's perspective, there is no logical reason for me to follow Christ. But I'm still fighting my guts out. I still want to know and follow Christ."

And then his cell phone chimes again—and another voice is calling him home:

> *"But now, GOD's Message, the God who made you in the first place, Jacob, the One who got you started, Israel: 'Don't be afraid, I've redeemed you. I've called your name. You're mine. When you're in over your head, I'll be there with you. When you're in rough waters, you will not go down. When you're between a rock and a hard place, it won't be a dead end— because I am GOD, your personal God, the Holy of*

Israel, your Savior. I paid a huge price for you:
all of Egypt, with rich Cush and Seba thrown in!
That's how much you mean to me! That's how much
I love you! I'd sell off the whole world to get you
back, trade the creation just for you.'"
ISAIAH 43:1–4 MSG

"When you're so lost and feel so alone and hopeless, all you hear from well-meaning folks is 'Blah, blah, blah,'" Keith says. "To help someone in my shoes, I would just tell them my story and not try to give them a bunch of advice. For me, my emotional black hole was so dark. I just had to get back up, keep breathing, and keep putting one foot right in front of the other.

"I eventually learned—again—that it's the Lord who sustains us. He keeps us coming back. Even though we fall again and again, we have to get back up. . .again and again. The Lord helps us in this way. Not because we deserve to be propped back up. The Lord is good and kind. He loves His children.

"The biggest lie that I still find myself falling for is the thought, *Even though I'm a child of God, He really doesn't want me. I am so absolutely messed up—just too far gone.* Sadly, this isn't past tense. I still struggle with these lies. But I keep moving forward. I keep praying. Sometimes I talk out loud while I'm driving. Sometimes I pray silently to the Lord. A lot of times in my heart, I'm yelling. A lot of times, I'm begging. And the Lord just keeps loving. He is 'God with me.' He is here and now. The Lord is near to the brokenhearted. He is closer to me now than ever before in my life."

12

HOW TO PRAY. . .
WHEN A PRODIGAL WANDERS

And the Father who knows all hearts knows what
the Spirit is saying, for the Spirit pleads for us
believers in harmony with God's own will.
ROMANS 8:27 NLT

People described Julie's mother as quiet and gentle. She was not
the kind of person who would demand to be heard or who would
want to be the center of attention. She rarely raised her voice.
She was humble and meek.

When she was blessed in Christ's presence, she didn't shout
aloud or dance in the aisles; she just quietly bowed her head and
cried.

Julie's mom would never think of praying loud or long in
public, yet her family knew she went frequently to her prayer
closet. Everyone could sense that she held an anointing from the
heavenly realm in her heart. In fact, people in grocery stores or
in waiting rooms—or anywhere the family would go—sought
her out and asked her to remember them in prayer. Strangers
asked for prayers of healing and salvation; prayers for sons and
daughters in the service or for prodigals far away from God.
People were drawn to her and to the Light she carried within.

Julie's father died unexpectedly at an early age, so her mother
was left to raise Julie and her younger sister on her own. While
the sister gave no one any trouble at all, Julie became a prodigal.
Despite her mother's love and a solid Christian upbringing, Julie

strayed from the faith. She attended church on Sundays, then lived a secret life outside of the sanctuary walls. Julie thought she had become an expert at fooling people with her dual roles. Yet her mother knew the truth all along. And her mother prayed without ceasing on her behalf.

"Lord, bring my prodigal child home," she'd cry out in her prayer closet. "Julie is hurting from the loss of her father. Have mercy on her, Lord! Put the desire to seek You above all things in her heart. Raise her up as a woman of God! Whatever it takes, Lord!"

> *So we have not stopped praying for you since we*
> *first heard about you. We ask God to give you*
> *complete knowledge of his will and to give you*
> *spiritual wisdom and understanding. Then the way*
> *you live will always honor and please the Lord,*
> *and your lives will produce every kind of good fruit.*
> *All the while, you will grow as you learn to*
> *know God better and better.*
> COLOSSIANS 1:9–10 NLT

Julie's mom often spoke the Word and believed—holding on to hope, the evidence of things not yet seen. Her faith had moved mountains. Still, her prodigal was far, far away.

Then the accident happened. A drunk driver hit the motorcycle on which Julie was riding, crushing her leg. She was rushed to emergency surgery, but the medical team was uncertain if her leg could be saved. Amputation was a very real possibility. Julie's mother went to prayer as a warrior to battle.

And the Holy Spirit helps us in our weakness.
For example, we don't know what God wants us
to pray for. But the Holy Spirit prays for us with
groanings that cannot be expressed in words.
ROMANS 8:26 NLT

In and out of consciousness over the next few days, Julie
remembered opening her eyes and seeing the sweet face of her
mother, who was at her bedside, smoothing her hair and holding
her hand. Even when Julie couldn't open her eyes, she could hear
her mother's prayers being whispered on her behalf. Prayers of
a saint were calling out to Jesus for Julie; the Word of God was
spoken over her body and soul.

And the Father who knows all hearts knows what
the Spirit is saying, for the Spirit pleads for us
believers in harmony with God's own will.
ROMANS 8:27 NLT

After several weeks of medical debate, the doctors decided not
to amputate Julie's leg—because, miraculously, it had begun to
heal! Her mother celebrated the answered prayer with tears. Then
she left Julie's room, walked down to the hospital chapel, and
worshipped Jesus.

But now, O Jacob, listen to the LORD who created
you. O Israel, the one who formed you says, "Do not
be afraid, for I have ransomed you. I have called you
by name; you are mine. When you go through deep
waters, I will be with you. When you go through

rivers of difficulty, you will not drown. When you
walk through the fire of oppression, you will not be
burned up; the flames will not consume you."
ISAIAH 43:1–2 NLT

Although the prayers for Julie's healing were answered, it was still several more years before her mother witnessed the fruit of her labor in prayer. Eventually, prayers to a praying saint brought Julie and her family back home—and into the heart of a spiritual awakening. God was in all the details, and Julie was privileged to be a part of a spiritual move of the Holy Spirit unlike any she had ever seen. Her life could not have been more blessed!

Were her mother's prayers answered? Absolutely! Did it happen overnight? Absolutely not.

Julie came home to the Father's house twenty-six years ago and has never left. Her desire to seek God in her life is stronger today than ever. She is devoted to being a woman of God. Her mother's prayers, spoken years ago, are still being answered. "God is faithful," Julie often tells others. "His promises are true."

Now to him who is able to do immeasurably
more than all we ask or imagine, according to his
power that is at work within us. . .
EPHESIANS 3:20

Today, Julie herself is a mother and she, too, has a prodigal child. Julie now knows of the magnitude and intensity of her mother's prayers over the years. And she, too, holds on to faith and assurance about what can't be seen—yet. However, she prays believing—not if but when!

Just like the father in the parable of the lost son, Julie stands waiting, watching into the distance for a first glimpse of her prodigal child on his way back home.

> *"While he was still a long way off, his father*
> *saw him and was filled with compassion*
> *for him. . . . So they began to celebrate."*
> LUKE 15:20, 24

Tips from the Prayer Closet

Remember the purpose of prayer. Prayer is meant to get you on track with God's will, not to adjust Him to your agenda. Here's how author Henry T. Blackaby explains it: "Prayer does not give you spiritual power. Prayer aligns your life with God so that He chooses to demonstrate His power through you. The purpose of prayer is not to convince God to change your circumstances, but to prepare you to be involved in God's activity."[1]

Expect results during prayer. Not only are we called to this divine activity (see Philippians 4:6 and 1 Timothy 2:1–3), but we are guaranteed God's action in response to our prayers. As 2 Chronicles 20:14–17 points out, God wants us to lay our anxieties before Him in prayer. He will take our worries and walk with us. He will carry our problems and give us peace. But remember, God responds *on His terms, according to His will,* and *in His perfect timing.* So if you've prayed and prayed without seeing the results you hoped for, maybe God has something else in mind. Refocus your prayers on what God wants to see happen in you.

13

HOW TO PRAY. . .
WHEN ALL IS CALM

Rejoice always, pray without ceasing, give thanks in all circumstances;
for this is the will of God in Christ Jesus for you.
—1 THESSALONIANS 5:16-18, ESV

Meet 54-year-old Vanessa from Long Island,
New York. This wife and ministry leader shares
in her own words her story—and how she strives
to pray continuously. . .not only when life gets
rough, but during seasons of peace, as well.

I have been following hard after Christ for more than forty-five years. I was raised a Christian home and gave my heart to the Lord at the early age of seven years of old. So naturally, my prayer life started at this young age. I was a very little girl way down here on earth, talking to a God who was way up in Heaven. I always wondered if He could really hear me from so far away. I mean, with everybody else He had to listen to, I just wasn't sure. But they were faithful prayers of a child who longed to know God and feel that He truly cared for me.

At first, my prayers were simple and were based on what I had been learned from my parents and Sunday School teachers. I didn't feel a strong connection, but I knew it was good to keep praying. I had grasped the concept that we were all separated from God and are in need of salvation. I had heard the story of Adam and Eve in the Garden and knew that our relationship with our creator was broken. But I didn't want it to be broken. I wanted to know God. So I kept praying to the big God in the sky, hoping He would hear me and answer me. The more I learned, as I went to church and read my Bible, the more I knew that He loved me and wanted me to be His child. But for years, I had no idea just how the depths of His love.

As I grew in life, and in my knowledge of God, I discovered a better understanding of prayer. For years I had been talking AT God. I would come before Him with request and concerns, asking Him for my desires. But during my pre-teen years, my prayer life changed when I realized that prayer is more of a conversation WITH God. I came to realize that He was always with me. This meant that I could speak with Him anytime, anywhere, about anything. He was safe to talk to. And as I began to share everything with Him, my trust in Him grew. I became more and more familiar with Him as my prayer life grew. He became my constant friend who was always there, loving and understanding me.

It's A Conversation

I attended a rough school during my early teen years. There was a lot of tension in the air and violence broke out in the blink of an eye. There were fights, riots, walkouts, and attacks on the staff. I'm sure the school office had the police on speed dial. And I was just a little girl with no idea of how to stand up for myself. I vividly remember the fear I felt as I began each school day. I was alone and scared. But I believed in God and I knew that I could pray, even in the mist of fear. I would often ask Him for help and wisdom throughout the day. I was fully aware that I was in over my head. I had no idea how to navigate my day that was full of uncertainty. So I spoke with the God who lived in my heart. The God that was with me every day, whether I was at home, church, or even school. This was when I began to hear from God. My prays had turned into more of a conversation. It began small, with little nudges and gut feelings. He began to open my eyes, and heart, as He guided my steps.

For example, I remember walking down the hall at school and suddenly feel the need to walk straight instead of turning down a different hallway. I wasn't looking around to see what was ahead. I just had a feeling. But I went with that feeling and continued to walk straight ahead. As I passed the hallway I had planned on walking down, I glanced over to see the danger I would have found if I had turned. It was that type of direction that God gave me throughout my day. I also remember asking God for a best friend or two. And that school year, I connected with a couple of other girls who were also trying to survive the school day, just like me. We became friends and would often stick up for each other. I was shocked. God had brought us together so we could face the mockery and danger of our day. They were resilient and brace as they stood up to the bullies. I was so thankful that He cared enough to meet the needs of this little girl in Junior High.

At my small church, where there were no other kids my age, I would sit alone or with my family. Most of the other kids sat in the back, whispering and passing notes. But I sat up front with my Bible and my notebook. Yep, I was a real Jesus geek. As I sat there and listened to the sermon, even at such young age, things would pop out at me from the Bible and from the sermon. I would take notes, writing down my questions and thoughts. My mind would wander as I thought about my life, my friends, and my school. I prayed for my friends a lot. So many times I would pray for those other girls at school while sitting through the service. These prayers helped my mind to open up to what God was trying to teach me. It made the sermons come alive. He would show me things that I would have never thought of on my own. And I did my best to write them down in my notebook so I could continue to think about them later.

It was very exciting to carry on a conversation with God like that, to ask Him questions and hear Him reply. I could feel His love and grace as we talked together. This sparked a desire in me to seek Him with my whole heart. I would write down my thoughts, my fears, my request, and the many questions I had about life. As God spoke to me during my prayer times, I would also write His words on the page. Sometimes they were words that focused on encouragement and assurances of His love for me. Other times He would lead me to a specific portion of scripture. His words in prayer, and His written words of the Bible, spoke directly to my needs. My relationship with God became more dynamic as He spoke to me in different ways. There were times when He would even drop simple bit of knowledge into my heart and mind - things I had no way of knowing on my own. Before, I prayed out of duty. But now, I prayed out of love. As this connection grew, I began to hear from Him more and more. I continued to write in my notebook as I prayed. The words would just seem to flow through my pencil. As He placed things on my heart, I would write them down. I cherished those words on the page. They were God's words, just for me. I learned that He wanted to speak to me even more than I wanted to speak to Him. It was the beginning of real communion with God. I was experiencing true fellowship with the One who is the lover of my soul. True communion. True prayer.

The Conversation Continues

Since then, I have learned the beauty of the Constant Conversation. That's right. I, just like you, have the ability to have an ongoing conversation with Jesus. The connection, that was birthed in the secret place, continues throughout our every day lives. As I spend time alone with my Creator, I soak in His love, forgiveness, and power that I carry with me. It is the beginning of a conversation that continues throughout my day. I rarely struggle to pray like I used to. What was once a mere discipline that was difficult to observe, is now a time of joy and peace. Sometimes I even wake from a deep sleep with a desire to join my Lord in prayer. Often, I spend my mornings in a quiet space that is reserved for God. I speak to Him there, not as a little girl talking to the God up in the sky, but as someone who is conversing with my Lord who is right there with me. His presence is full and powerful. Then, as I step into the routine of my life, I'm different. I can feel Him with me everywhere I go. His Spirit is living in me.

It is a beautiful gift we have been given…a personal, intimate relationship with our Creator, the God of the Universe. When I speak to Him I know He is not somewhere far away looking down on me from a distance. But He lives in me and breathes through me since the very first day I invited Him into my heart as a young child.

I have continued to journal in my little notebooks throughout the years. And He continues to make and keep His promises. This Continual Conversation is birthed in my alone times with Him. I love Him with my words, my songs, and even in my silence. It is a connection that will last throughout eternity.

Check It Out

So how do I know I'm hearing from God? How do I know it's not just my own thoughts and ideas? I have learned to seek God's Word for guidance. I have faith that He isn't going to guide me outside of His character. He's not going to lead me into actions for beliefs that are contrary to His very nature. God has given us more than one way to know Him. And as I grow in prayer, studying His Word, and being a part of His family, I see more and more how these things work together. When I hear, feel, or gain insight, I need to know that I am receiving them from the Lord. I just like to know from where they originate. How can I know if my thoughts are His thoughts?

- Are my thoughts from God? If something from the world around me sparks a thought or idea, it may or may not be from Him. Come before Him in prayer and ask for clarification. If these ideas are Godly in nature and point me to Jesus, He will reinforce them. If they help strengthen my love for God, then I should consider it wisdom that should be incorporated into my life. If they remind me to praise my Lord, then praise should readily follow. God created our world. He can, and does, use our surroundings to draw us closer to Him.

- What if my thoughts seem to come from my emotions? Take some advice from King David. He asked God to search his heart and show him the things that are hidden. Long before he became king, David brought his struggles to the Lord through prayer and praise. You too can ask God to bring those hidden things to light and give you the courage to see the things that He wants you to work on. Emotions aren't bad. They are a natural and God given. And they are also a tool used to identify a need or desire. So many negative emotions are rooted in deeply hidden hurts and fears. So don't ignore emotions as a silly nascence of life. God loves to work in our emotions. They are often avenues that God uses to help us dig deeper and draw closer in Him.

- What if my ideas don't make sense? This is a critical time to seek clarity. Again, God will not lead you to act outside of His character. At the same time, we must remember that His ways are not often practiced in our world. Even in the life of a believer, we tend to seek our own will. So He will most likely lead you to act outside of your norm. What makes sense in our world, and our own minds, is often contrary to the ways of the Lord. So check your thoughts with Scripture. Pray for guidance and wisdom. Ask others to join you in prayer. Because God brings us into community with others so we can share in this life journey. He places people in our lives to help us grow and serve one another. Common sense doesn't always prevail. But God's perfect love always leads us to decisions that glorify Him. And in that, we are blessed.

- Who should I ask for help? We were created to live in community with God, and with others. He created us to multiply and share life together. And He works through this system to help us know Him better. Seek out Godly people who are also seeking His will. Spend time praying together. Open your Bibles and learn from Him, together. And open yourself up to listening to the thoughts and ideas of those who are wise in their faith. God has often spoken to me through others. Through them, He can clarify His Word in my life. I can't afford to be a lone ranger. We really do need each other.

Experiencing God

Life is full of surprises. Sometimes they are small and insignificant. And other times they are huge and life changing. It is during the every day life that my relationship with Christ has developed. It is the every day desire to seek Him and His ways that shapes my life. My continual conversation, reading His Word, and seeking Godly advice, is the foundation of my spiritual development. God works in these ways to teach me and train me. As my faith continues to grow, I begin to see the world through His eyes. My heart begins to have compassion for those that are often overlooked. His insights bring me into a better understanding of who He is and who I am in Him. Then when the big life struggles happen, I'm already in sync with my Lord. That type of spiritual maturity cannot be gained in the middle of a crisis. But it is revealed in a moment of crisis.

God is closer, kinder, bigger, and more loving that we can ever imagine. And for years, my prayers have been too small. I have made Him too small, and too far away. But through the guidance of His Word and some really good teachers, I am learning about real faith. It's powerful and beautiful. It's about a life of seeking and learning that never ends. We have been offered a life of freedom and forgiveness. He has paid the price for our salvation. We just need to step inside into that promise and embrace it. Grab a hold of it and squeeze. Long for His holiness in the deepest places of your life. It's not always an emotional experience or a spiritual high. A life of faith is often found in the small steady persistence of our daily lives. It's a lifestyle of dedication and devotion. So much of our growth comes during those quiet and calm moments. Don't miss the opportunity to connect with Him today. Go, seek, and receive.

14

HOW TO PRAY. . .
WHEN YOU DON'T KNOW HOW

I (Arnie) see brokenness all around me. In my own town—
a relatively affluent Nebraska community—children and homeless
families go hungry. Some huddle near busy intersections, clutching
tattered signs: NEED FOOD. UNEMPLOYED VET. HELP MY FAMILY.
Teens who look more like streetwalkers and gangbangers file into
our schools. I flip on the news, and I'm assaulted by a barrage of
nonstop misery: rising gas prices, crashing markets; earthquakes
along the Pacific Rim, tornadoes in the Midwest. "Terrorists
mastermind another bombing. . ." "Scandal on Capitol Hill. . ."
"A deadly shooting inside a mega-church. . ."

Man's inhumanity toward man. Fractured families. Broken
hearts.

Lying. Cheating. Stealing. Anger. Envy. Gossip. Greed.
Pride. Sin.

Everywhere. All around us and in us—you, me, our children.
No one is immune. Yet on most days we manage to stay pretty
numb to it all. "We ignore our failures and downplay our moral
meltdowns," writes author Steven James. "We fill our lives with
frantic distractions so we can avoid noticing the splinter of guilt
embedded so deeply in our souls."[1]

Making sense of such a senseless world can feel overwhelm-
ing at times. How should I pray in the middle of the mess? How
can I help? Standing by helplessly as others suffer is especially
hard. How on earth did life end up this way?

I guess the deeper question is, why do we all have a splinter
in our souls?

Genesis 3 tells us *what* happened in the garden: *The serpent shows up, a lie about God is whispered, a soul-robbing choice is made, forbidden fruit is tasted, and then—BAM!—humans are tossed into the thorns of a fallen world.*

Yet Adam and Eve were made in the image of God, and an image represents someone or something. So on earth, they *represented* the Lord. They had every advantage to succeed: a perfect home, a perfect purpose, a perfect relationship.

So why did they end up immobilized by temptation and felled by sin? Why did such a perfect beginning for humanity degenerate into the chaos we experience today?

Two reasons.

We Are Free to Choose

God didn't create us to be human automatons. Instead, the One who uttered neutrons into existence gave His greatest masterpieces the freedom to dream, to use their imaginations, and to think on their own. They were free to work with their hands and to create. They were free to make their own decisions and to govern the world on God's behalf. But in doing so, the Lord exposed Himself to the pain of jilted love.[2] Adam and Eve could choose to *love* God and to become clearer images of Him. . .or they could choose to turn their backs on Him and *reject* Him altogether.

God could have existed for all of eternity without pain, but instead He risked anguish in order to have someone outside Himself to love; someone who would freely love Him back.[3] And this is the genius of God's creation.

Yale University's Karen C. Hinckley explains it this way in her book *The Story of Stories: The Bible in Narrative Form*:

He [God] had previously made creatures who
were pure spirit: They could reason, make choices,
and perceive qualities in God like His majesty.
"Holy, holy, holy!" they cried as they worshiped Him
unceasingly for His greatness and perfection. But
His love was beyond their capacity to grasp. A being
needed feelings—even passion—to understand
what it would mean to offer oneself to another
vulnerably and to share—well, to share love.
God was a passionate, self-giving Being, and His
angels were utterly unable to appreciate this side
of Him. On the other side, animals had feelings
but could not reason and make moral choices; their
love lacked consciousness and maturity. Man was
God's ingenious hybrid—spirit and soul, reason and
passion, the finest reflection of Himself that God
could produce.[4]

And so, to practice their Godlike qualities of creativity and
authority, Adam and Eve were put in charge of the garden. To
practice their ability to make moral choices, they received one
restriction: Don't eat from the Tree of the Knowledge of Good
and Evil.

But an invader from outside the physical universe, a spirit
who camouflaged himself as a serpent, tempted Eve: "For God
knows that when you eat from it your eyes will be opened,
and you will be like God, knowing good and evil" (Genesis
3:4–5). In other words, *He doesn't really love you. He wants to
keep you ignorant and under His thumb, abiding by an endless list
of unreasonable rules. You're more like an amusing pet than a person.*

Rebellion is your only choice.

Adam and Eve had no idea that the imposter had been the highest of God's angelic servants until he rebelled. According to tradition, his name had been Lucifer ("lightbearer"), but it became Satan ("the adversary") and Abaddon ("the destroyer"). He simply did not care to spend eternity worshipping his Creator; he considered that boring and beneath him. So he declared his independence and set up a rival kingdom.[5]

The serpent was crafty. He knew how to sway the minds of the world's first couple. *Does God really know what's best for you? Could you be happier looking out for yourselves instead of always listening to Him?*

The scent and color of the forbidden fruit enticed the man and woman's senses, and suddenly, everything they knew about the Lord—His desire for them, His loving care, His wisdom and gentleness—all was forgotten. At that moment, truth was traded for lies. As they gave in to temptation and were dragged into rebellion against God, a deadly menace was freed, one that would taunt and toy with humans until the end of time.

We Ache for Control

Deep in our heart of hearts, we all want to call the shots for ourselves.

I'm going to live my *life* my *way—carve out* my *place in this world, find meaning, and get the things that satisfy* me. Sometimes we even mouth the lies that Satan whispered in the garden: *I'm just not ready to fully trust God. I mean, how can I be sure that He really cares about me and my problems? If He does, then where is He? Why can't I hear Him? Maybe I really would be happier doing things my way.*

Yet our preoccupation with *me*—and not God—is exactly

what went wrong in the garden. Adam and Eve rejected that one single command that God had given them, and all of human history changed. They bought that lie from Satan: they became convinced that being in charge of their own souls was best. The only problem with that strategy is that we humans tend to make bad choices. Part of the reason we make bad choices is that we don't see the entire picture, the complete story. But another reason is that we are simply selfish. Since the fall, self-centeredness—not God-centeredness—has become the defining characteristic of our lives.

"Governing the cosmos on God's behalf was—and is—not enough for humanity," writes author and Bible expert Scot McKnight. "Humans ache to rule the cosmos. They want to be God. The ache to be God and acting as if we are God are what sin is all about."[6]

Even though there is plenty of evidence through the ages that mankind's view of good and evil is flawed, we still want to be in control. Isn't this how most of us live our lives? Control appeals to our baser instincts. Yet we are *not* masters of our fate or captains of our own souls. Like it or not, sin leads us down all kinds of deadly paths:

- We allow our will to usurp the power of God.
- We redefine sin and morality: "There is a way that appears to be right, but in the end it leads to death" (Proverbs 14:12).
- We base our significance (and the status of others) on attributes such as strength, beauty, intelligence, achievements, wealth.
- We seek happiness anywhere but the Source: our own pleasures and pastimes, alcohol and drugs, sports and

gambling, vacations, money, houses, pets, possessions.

- We seek love anywhere but the Source: human relationships, lust, sex.
- We seek meaning anywhere but the Source: careers, religious practices, power.

∾

Think about a typical day. Much of it is spent trying to make life work *without* God in the center. Yet we still expect Him to cooperate with us—relating to us on *our* terms, revolving around *our* plans, solving problems so we can live the way *we want to live*. And while we may think our lives are humming along just fine, we are deceived. Gradually, choice by choice, a chasm between us and God grows wider and deeper.

Becoming disconnected from the Source is lethal.

Simply put, separation from the Lord is *the* root cause of everything that has gone wrong (and will go wrong) in our lives. It's the cause of that splinter that's so deeply embedded in our souls. Which brings us back to the question I asked earlier: Why?

"Why is it so easy to listen to the whisperings of a snake and so hard to hear the voice of the Lamb?" asks Steven James. "Why are we drawn so naturally to illusion and so slow to pursue the truth? I think it's because ever since Adam and Eve's fatal choice, the jargon of temptation has been our natural tongue and the dialect of love has been a foreign language."[7]

∾

Yep, I see brokenness all around me. Sin is everywhere. All around us and *in* us—you, me, our children. So what can I do about it?

Live.

Love.

Pray.

And when I don't know exactly what to pray or how to begin. . .

I pray the Psalms—especially the words of King David:
>Teach me your ways, O LORD, that I may live according to your truth! Grant me purity of heart, so that I may honor you. With all my heart I will praise you, O Lord my God. I will give glory to your name forever, for your love for me is very great. You have rescued me from the depths of death. (Psalm 86:11–13 NLT)

I pray the prayers of other believers passed down through the ages:
>Almighty God, our heavenly Father, who settest the solitary in families: We commend to thy continual care the homes in which thy people dwell. Put far from them, we beseech thee, every root of bitterness, the desire of vainglory, and the pride of life. Fill them with faith, virtue, knowledge, temperance, patience, godliness. Knit together in constant affection those who, in holy wedlock, have been made one flesh. Turn the hearts of the parents to the children, and the hearts of the children to the parents; and so enkindle fervent charity among us all, that we may evermore be kindly affectioned one to another; through Jesus Christ our Lord. Amen.[8]

I pray exactly the words Jesus taught us to pray:

"Our Father in heaven, hallowed be your name, your kingdom come, your will be done, on earth as it is in heaven. Give us today our daily bread. And forgive us our debts, as we also have forgiven our debtors. And lead us not into temptation, but deliver us from the evil one" (Matthew 6:9–13).

ENDNOTES

INTRODUCTION

1. David Watson, *Called and Committed: World-Changing Discipleship* (Wheaton, IL: Harold Shaw, 1982), 82.
2. Ibid., 83.
3. Kay Arthur, *Lord, Teach Me to Pray in 28 Days* (Eugene, OR: Harvest House, 1982),

CHAPTER 1: A PEEK INSIDE YOUR CLOSET:
PRAYER LIVES OF EVERYDAY CHRISTIANS

1. Pamela Caudill Ovwigho and Arnie Cole, "Faith in Real Life: An In-Depth Look at the Spiritual Lives of People around the Globe," September 2011, http://www.backtothebible.org/files/web/docs/cbe/Faith_in_Real_Life_In_Depth_Look_at_Spiritual_Lives_around_Globe.pdf.

2. Patricia Barnes et al., *CDC Advance Data Report #343: Complementary and Alternative Medicine Use among Adults: United States, 2002.* Washington, DC: National Center for Complementary and Alternative Medicine, 2002.

3. Mary Fran Tracy et al., "Use of Complementary and Alternative Therapies: A National Survey of Critical Care Nurses." *American Journal of Critical Care* 14 (2005): 404–14.

4. Kevin Masters and Glen Spielmans, "Prayer and Health: Review, Meta-analysis, and Research Agenda." *Journal of Behavioral Medicine* 30 (2007): 329–38.

5. Andrew Newberg, "How God Changes Your Brain: An Introduction to Jewish Neurotheology," *CCAR Journal: The Reform Jewish Quarterly* (2016): 18–25.

6. Adapted from Clay Routledge, "5 Scientifically Supported Benefits of Prayer," June 23, 2014, https://www.psychologytoday.com/blog/more-mortal/201406/5-scientifically-supported-benefits-prayer.

CHAPTER 2: BUT GOD RARELY SHOWS UP...SO
WHY PRAY?

1. Billy Graham, *Peace with God* (Garden City, NY: Doubleday, 1953), 160.
2. Seattle pastor and writer Greg Asimakoupoulos contributed to this chapter.
3. Warren W. Wiersbe, *On Earth as It Is in Heaven* (Grand Rapids: Baker Books, 2010), 118.
4. Sarah Lebhar Hall, "Why God Lets Us Stay Weak," *Christianity Today*, May 2016, 51.
5. Tony Jones, *Pray* (Colorado Springs: NavPress, 2003), 31.

CHAPTER 3: HOW PRAYER WORKS

1. R. C. Sproul, *Effective Prayer* (Wheaton, IL: Tyndale, 1984).

2. Johnson Oatman, "Count Your Blessings," 1897 (public domain).

3. Andrew Murray, *Humility: The Journey toward Holiness* (Minneapolis: Bethany House, 2001), 103.

4. David Watson, *Called and Committed: World-Changing Discipleship* (Wheaton, IL: Harold Shaw, 1982), 83.

5. Henry T. Blackaby and Richard Blackaby, *Experiencing God Day-by-Day Devotional* (Nashville: Broadman & Holman, 1998), 360.

6. Margaret Magdalen, *Jesus, Man of Prayer* (Downers Grove, IL: InterVarsity, 1987), 51.

Chapter 4: Confession: Regaining Intimacy with God

1. "Mark" and "Ashley" are pseudonyms. Their names were changed to protect their identities. Portions of this story are adapted from Arnie Cole and Michael Ross, *Tempted, Tested, True* (Minneapolis: Bethany House, 2013), 165–74.
2. C. S. Lewis, *Mere Christianity* (San Francisco: Harper San Francisco, 1952), 32.
3. Patrick A. Means, *Men's Secret Wars* (Grand Rapids: Revell, 1999), 176.
4. Ibid., 177–78.
5. Ibid., 225–26.
6. Robert S. McGee, *The Search for Significance Student Edition* (Nashville: W Publishing Group, 2003), 105.
7. Max Lucado, *He Still Moves Stones* (Nashville: Word, 1993), 110.
8. Ibid.

CHAPTER 5: THE SECRET OF VICTORIOUS LIVING

1. Encyclopædia Britannica Online, Encyclopædia Britannica Inc., 2012, http://www.britannica.com/EBchecked/topic/168802/Domitian.

2. Karen C. Hinckley, *The Story of Stories: The Bible in Narrative Form* (Colorado Springs: NavPress, 1991), 327.

3. See Matthew 7:15–23.

4. Hinckley, *Story of Stories*, 328.

5. Dr. Larry Crabb, *66 Love Letters: A Conversation with God that Invites You into His Story* (Nashville: Thomas Nelson, © 2009), 375.

6. Ibid., Matthew 4:3.

7. Walter Wangerin Jr., *The Book of God* (Grand Rapids: Zondervan, 1996), 623.

8. Ted Miller, *The Story* (Wheaton, IL: Tyndale, 1986), 316.

9. This retelling of Jesus' temptation is adapted from Michael Ross, *Tribe: A Warrior's Heart* (Carol Stream, IL: Tyndale, 2004), 89–90.

10. Billy Graham, *Peace with God* (Garden City, NY: Doubleday, 1953), 161.

11. Rich Mullins, quoted in Les Sussman, *Praise Him! Christian Music Stars Share Their Favorite Verses from Scripture* (New York: St. Martin's Press, 1998), 155–64.

CHAPTER 6: FIFTY FACTS ABOUT PRAYER, THE BIBLE, FAITH, AND SPIRITUAL GROWTH

1. Barbara Bradley Hagerty, "Prayer May Reshape Your Brain. . . and Your Reality," NPR website, February 25, 2011, http://www.npr.org/templates/story/story.php?storyId=104310443.
2. Jake Whitman, "Power of Prayer: What Happens to Your Brain When You Pray," NBC News website, March 22, 2016, http://www.nbcnews.com/news/religion/power-prayer-what-happens-your-brain-when-you-pray-n273956.

CHAPTER 8: LEARNING FROM THE LORD'S PRAYER

1. R. T. Kendall, *The Lord's Prayer* (Grand Rapids: Chosen Books, 2010), 29.
2. Max Lucado, *The Great House of God* (Nashville: Word, 1997), 36.
3. Kendall, *Lord's Prayer*, 38–39.
4. Warren W. Wiersbe, *On Earth as It Is in Heaven* (Grand Rapids: Baker Books, 2010), 11.
5. C. S. Lewis, *Mere Christianity, Book I: Right and Wrong as a Clue to the Meaning of the Universe* (London: Macmillan, 1952), 22.
6. Tony Jones, *Pray* (Colorado Springs: NavPress, 2003), 92.
7. Warren W. Wiersbe, *On Earth as It Is in Heaven* (Grand Rapids: Baker Books, 2010), 93.
8. Ibid., 92.
9. Charles F. Stanley, *When the Enemy Strikes* (Nashville: Thomas Nelson, 2004), 6.

CHAPTER 9: PRAYING THE PSALMS

1. Kenneth Barker, general editor, *The NIV Study Bible* (Grand Rapids: Zondervan, 1985), 782.

2. Jeanne Guyon, *Experiencing the Depths of Jesus Christ*, ed. Gene Edwards (Goleta, CA: Christian Books, 1975). 62.

CHAPTER 10: HISTORY'S FAMOUS PRAYERS

1. John Bunyan, *A Book for Boys and Girls, or Temporal Things Spiritualized* (London: Printed for and sold by R. Tookey at his printing house in St. Christopher's Court, in Threadneedle Street, behind the Royal Exchange, 1701), 8.

2. Quoted in Dorothy M. Stewart, *The Westminster Collection of Christian Prayers* (Louisville: Westminster John Knox, 2002), 303.

3. Malcolm Muggeridge, from *The Communion of Saints: Prayers of the Famous,* ed. Horton Davies (Grand Rapids: Eerdmans, 1990).

4. "St. Patrick's Breastplate, the Poem of Ireland's Greatest Saint," IrishCentral Website, 2016, http://www.irishcentral.com/roots/St-Patricks-breastplate-the-poem-of-Irelands-greatest-saint-.html.

5. Ogden Nash, quoted in "Morning Prayers," compiled by Richard A. Kauffman, February 1, 2006, *Christianity Today,* http://www.christianitytoday.com/ct/2006/february/32.86.html. Kauffman excerpted the prayer by Ogden Nash from David Yount, *Breaking Through God's Silence* (New York: Simon & Schuster, 1996).

6. Dietrich Bonhoeffer, quoted in Stewart, *Westminster Collection of Christian Prayers,* 278.

7. "Prayers by Mother Teresa of Calcutta," Christian Miracles website, 2008–2016, http://www.christian-miracles.com/motherteresasprayers.htm.

8. Thomas à Kempis, quoted in Stewart, *Westminster Collection of Christian Prayers*, 183.

9. Shane Claiborne, Jonathan Wilson-Hartgrove, and Enuma Okoro, *Common Prayer: A Liturgy for Ordinary Radicals* (Grand Rapids: Zondervan, 2010), 337.

10. "John Wesley's 'Covenant Prayer,'" Beliefnet, http://www.beliefnet.com/columnists/prayerplainandsimple/2010/02/john-wesleys-covenant-prayer-1.html.

11. Mark Gilroy, *Pocket Book of Prayers* (New York: Fall River Press, 2015), 41–42.

12. "Prayers for Families and Personal Life," *The Book of Common Prayer* (New York: Oxford University Press, 2007), 828–29.

13. "A Prayer for His Son by Gen. Douglas MacArthur," posted by differencemakersblogspot.com Thursday, May 12, 2005.

14. Janet Lees, "God of Good Ideas," in *Seeing Christ in Others*, ed. Geoffrey Duncan (Norwich: Canterbury Press, 1998).

CHAPTER 12: HOW TO PRAY. . .WHEN A
PRODIGAL WANDERS
1.   Henry T. Blackaby and Richard Blackaby,
     Experiencing God Day-by-Day Devotional
     (Nashville: Broadman & Holman, 1998), 20.

CHAPTER 14: HOW TO PRAY. . .WHEN YOU DON'T
KNOW HOW

1. Steven James, *Story: Recapture the Mystery* (Grand Rapids: Revell, 2006), 20.
2. See Karen C. Hinckley, *The Story of Stories: The Bible in Narrative Form* (Colorado Springs: NavPress, 1991), 15.
3. Ibid.
4. Ibid.
5. See ibid., 16–17.
6. Scot McKnight, "Why Doesn't Anybody Talk about Sin?" *Relevant,* July 13, 2011, http://www.relevantmagazine.com/god/deeper-walk/features/26172-why-doesnt-anybody-talk-about-sin-anymore.
7. James, *Story,* 89.
8. "Prayers for Families and Personal Life," *The Book of Common Prayer* (New York: Oxford University Press, 2007), 828–29.

IF YOU ENJOYED THIS BOOK ON PRAYER, HERE ARE TWO MORE YOU'LL ENJOY...

Dangerous Prayer

Join gifted speaker and award-winning author, Cheri Fuller, as she illustrates—from Bible times to today—what happens when God's people pray dangerous prayers. Each of the 21 chapters is rooted in scripture and weaves together a beautiful tapestry of lives and kingdoms impacted through the power of prayer.

Paperback / 978-1-63409-115-2 / $14.99

Fresh Encounter with Jesus

In *Fresh Encounters with Jesus*, Cheri Fuller shares stories of biblical and historical figures, modern believers, and her own journey of faith. She shows how God comes to us through the Bible, service, trials, mountaintop experiences, and even quiet whispers. Fuller's stories will encourage women to fall in love with the Lord anew and live life with gratefulness and trust.

Paperback / 978-1-63058-352-1 / $7.99